The Doctrine
of
SALVATION

Darrell W. Robinson

CONVENTION PRESS

Nashville, Tennessee

5420-93XM

This book is the text for course 05-096
in the subject area Baptist Doctrine
in the Church Study Course

Dewey Decimal Classification: 234
Subject Heading: SALVATION

Printed in the United States of America

Discipleship Training Department
The Sunday School Board
of the Southern Baptist Convention
127 Ninth Avenue, North
Nashville, Tennessee 37234

Contents

About the Author

DARRELL W. ROBINSON has a rich and varied background in ministry. A graduate of Baylor University and Southwestern Baptist Theological Seminary, he earned his doctorate from Luther Rice Theological Seminary. He was also awarded an honorary doctorate by Houston Baptist University.

Robinson has served as the pastor of several churches in Texas, Kansas, and Alabama. His pastorates include First Baptist Church in Vernon, Texas; First Baptist Church in Pasadena, Texas; and Dauphin Way Baptist Church in Mobile, Alabama. He is widely known as an evangelist and a conference speaker. Robinson joined the Home Mission Board of the Southern Baptist Convention in May 1989. As the vice-president, evangelism, Home Mission Board, he influences all Southern Baptists in the area of evangelism.

Robinson and his wife, Kathy, reside in the Atlanta area. They have four children: Duane Robinson, Lori Winston, Robin Robinson, and Loren Robinson. The Robinsons have two grandchildren: Matthew and Blakely.

Preface

SALVATION from start to finish is the work of God. God's abounding grace overshadows all creation to reveal His love and salvation in Christ to every person. To God be the glory for His purpose of salvation in taking the initiative to provide the Lamb, slain before the foundation of the world. To Him be eternal praise for sending His Son to become sin for us so we might be made the righteousness of God in Him. To Him be our love and commitment for giving His Word and Spirit to grow us into Christlikeness and to deliver us into His presence in heaven. To Him be thanksgiving with fullness of joy for the privilege of being part of the body of Christ on mission to take the gospel of His salvation to every person.

To God be honor for the church triumphant and for the ultimate victory, through which He has made us "more than conquerors through him that loved us" (Rom. 8:37). To God—Father, Son, and Holy Spirit—be glory, praise, and thanksgiving with joy, commitment, and honor because He is God.

Acknowledgments

I WANT to acknowledge my deep appreciation to my devoted wife, Kathy, who has labored faithfully with me through the years as I formulated my understanding of the concepts in this book. She assisted diligently in the assimilation of material and gave of herself to enable me to have time to write. Most of all, her commitments to her Lord and to her husband have been undergirding sources of inspiration. Her statement to me in a critical time of decision for our ministry was "I have committed myself to God to do whatever He desires so He can use you in the greatest way possible."

My debt is great to the churches with whom I have been privileged to minister as pastor and in evangelism. They have provided climates for growth and opportunities to implement our Lord's mission.

I am grateful for the assistance of my secretary, Virginia Whitehead, who read this material and offered suggestions, and to Pat Mills and Gena Lamar, who typed the manuscript. I am grateful for the supportive and encouraging Home Mission Board staff, on which I have the joy of serving.

The Human Condition

QUESTIONS TO GUIDE YOUR STUDY
1. *What does it mean to say that a person is lost?*
2. *How can human accomplishment and goodness on the part of the unsaved be explained?*
3. *What are the consequences of being lost in this life? in eternity?*

On a Saturday morning I stopped by to see Carl, a 92-year-old lost man. In the course of our conversation I decided to take a direct approach in dealing with Carl about his spiritual condition. I started by saying, "May I ask you a personal question?"

"Sure," he replied.

"Are you a saved man, Carl? Has God saved you?"

"Oh, yes, I have been saved twice. Once when I was eight years old, I was alone on our farm. A man came along, picked me up, and held me by my head over a well. He was going to drop me into the well, but suddenly he put me down. God saved me!

"The other time I was working at a chemical plant. I was leaving work when an explosion occurred where I had been working. I had left just in time. God saved me!"

"That is wonderful, Carl. God saved you twice physically so that He could save you spiritually," I responded. "May I tell you how you can be saved spiritually and eternally?"

After I explained the gospel of Christ, Carl prayed and received Him. He joyfully followed Christ in baptism and active church membership. Carl had been lost, but God saved him.

To understand the need for salvation, it is necessary to take a comprehensive look at sin and its tragic effects on humanity. Sin resulted in humanity's lostness. Apart from this realization, salvation is meaningless.

The word *salvation* comes from the Greek word *soteria*, which means *deliverance*. Spiritually, it is our deliverance from sin and death to forgiveness and life. *Save (sozo)* is the act and process of deliverance. *Savior (soter)* is the person who has accomplished our deliverance. Jesus is the essential part of God's plan of salvation.

Certainly, as in Carl's case, God in His providential care acts in physical deliverance of people. But the need of humankind and the great work of God are salvation from sin and lostness. God addressed humans need in the person and work of Jesus Christ.

The word of the angel of the Lord to Joseph was " 'She will give birth to a son, and you are to give him the name Jesus, because he will save his people from their sins' " (Matt. 1:21, NIV).[1]

Lost in Sin: The Human Situation

Jesus stated the purpose of His coming to this world: "The Son of man is come to seek and to save that which was lost" (Luke 19:10). One of the great needs of the church in accomplishing its mission for Christ is to rediscover what it means to be lost. Multitudes, even believers, have lost sight of lostness.

It does not take long for a Christian to forget what it was like to be lost. A rebellious man came to Christ. He was gloriously saved. He had resisted the witness of the Lord through his wife and other Christians for a long time. One week after he was saved, he came to his pastor with a deep concern for a friend.

He said: "I have been telling Sammy about Jesus, but he is not interested. I just don't understand what is wrong with Sammy."

The young Christian had already forgotten what it is like to be lost. The lost are sentenced to spiritual death as a consequence of sin. Romans 5:12 declares, "Just as sin entered the world through one man, and death through sin, and in this way death came to all men, because all sinned" (NIV).

When Adam sinned, spiritual death and separation came into the human race. A barrier of sin came between God and humans as the result of human sin: "Jews and Gentiles alike are all under sin" (Rom. 3:9, NIV).

God is holy. God is *above* sin. Humankind is sinful individually and as a race. Humans are *under* sin. The sin barrier is impenetrable, as far as humans are concerned. They cannot penetrate the sin barrier and reach God.

Positionally, all humankind is under sin, separated from God, and lost. Humanity is a fallen race. The entire human race is lost without hope except for God's intervention to penetrate the sin barrier and to provide a way for people to come to Him. Every person is born into a race that is under sin.

Personally, every individual is under sin's dominion and authority: "All have sinned and fall short of the glory of God" (Rom. 3:23, NIV). Sin has so affected every person that he or she possesses an inherent tendency toward evil, resulting in attitudes and acts of disobedience to God. Sin is a disease of the character that humans cannot cure. Sin is a flaw in personality that humans cannot correct.

PERSONAL LEARNING ACTIVITY 1

Underline the phrase that best completes the following statement.

Wrong attitudes and acts of obedience toward God result from (a lack of education, impossible demands by God, human sinfulness).

Since Adam introduced sin into the world, with its resultant separation and death, one might point a finger of blame at him and not accept personal responsibility and guilt. The fact is that all by choice have sinned and are responsible. To argue the opposite is of no avail: "that every mouth may be silenced and the whole world held accountable to God" (Rom. 3:19, NIV). The individual is responsible for his own sin.

Theologians speak of the depravity of human beings. What does this mean? Total depravity means that—

all men (including those who are moral and religious) are sinners. But that does not mean that there is no difference between an Albert Schweitzer and an Adolf Hitler. It would be absurd to say that since, according to Jesus, a man who lusts is guilty of adultery, there is no difference between a "girl watcher" and a rapist. Or that there is no difference between a man who is angry with his neighbor and a man who shoots his neighbor. The extreme statements in the confessions do not mean that all men are monsters or devils, or that all men are equally "bad." . . .

Total depravity, correctly understood, means that although both Christians *and* non-Christians can do much good, no part of any man's being (body, mind, soul or spirit) and nothing he does (including very moral, heroic or religious acts) are free from the corruption of sin. It means that although there may be all kinds of progress in history, man himself stays monotonously the same."[2]

Sin's dominion has made humanity its slave. "This sinful condition is a trap from which we cannot free ourselves no matter how heroic the effort."[3] The entire being of sinful humans is tainted with self-interest. The root of sin is selfishness. A person without Christ centers his life in himself rather than in God. In the garden Adam and Eve acted on the basis of their own desires rather than the will of God. Sin in any life is rebellion against the will of God.

The Bible defines *sin* as *missing the mark* (Greek *hamartano*; see Rom. 3:23). The word pictures an archer aiming an arrow at a target, representing God's will, character, and glory. The arrow comes short—misses the mark—of the glory of God. Sin manifests itself in transgression of the law of God (see Jas. 2:9-11; 1 John 3:4) and disobedience (see Eph. 2:2). Such words as *iniquity, wickedness, lawlessness, vile affections, offense,* and *crookedness* describe sin. The greatest and most condemning sin is that of unbelief in Jesus Christ (see John 3:18) because Jesus Christ is God's ultimate expression of love. To reject Him is to choose one's own way instead of God's only provision for human sin.

In the early chapters of the Book of Romans Paul presented convincing arguments about the universality of sin. Some human reasoning suggests that humankind is evolving toward perfection. Certainly, there is evidence that the human family has made great progress in many areas. The high-tech society of the late 20th century is evidence of humankind's progress. In everything from space travel to modern medical science it is clear that the human family has made great strides.

Yet, as Paul reasoned in Romans 1, human progress has not brought human beings into a right relationship with God. As a matter of fact, Paul painted a grim picture of spiritual devolution rather than spiritual evolution.

Romans 1 shows six steps of the downward movement of sin. First is indifference to the general revelation of God to humankind. As a result, humans are without excuse (see Rom. 1:19-20). Second, ingratitude causes humans not to glorify God and results in foolish, darkened hearts (see Rom. 1:21). Third, irrationality causes humans to elevate themselves in pride, therefore rejecting the thought of God (see Rom. 1:22-23). Fourth, immorality becomes the life-style as God gives humans over to the uncleanness of their sinful desires (see Rom. 1:24). Fifth, idolatry becomes the expression of a life that has a capacity for God but has rejected Him. Thus, humans with their incurable yearning for God create their own gods, attempting vainly to fill the vacuum in their lives. They worship and serve the creation instead of the Creator (see Rom. 1:25). Sixth, infidelity in all of life's relationships characterizes human existence. Paul listed a series of vile and hideous sins against God and society that result when humans reject God and God gives them over to depraved minds (see Rom. 1:26-32).

P E R S O N A L   L E A R N I N G   A C T I V I T Y   2

Write one sentence to explain what the author means when he says that Paul pictured human spiritual devolution rather than spiritual evolution.

_____

_____

_____

_____

Lost in Sin: Biblical Descriptions

The horrifying description of those who are lost permeates the pages of the Scriptures from Genesis to Revelation. It begins in the garden with the guilty pair running from God and attempting to hide from His presence. All humankind has followed suit. It ends in the Book of Revelation with humans deifying humans, shaking a fist of rebellion in the face of God to institute human-centered worship. Herschel H. Hobbs has graphically analyzed Paul's discourse on the universal sinfulness and lostness of man in Romans 3:10-18.[4] First, in verses 10-12 Paul looked at sin through the eyes of a philosopher:

> As it is written:
> "There is no one righteous, not even one;
>   there is no one who understands,
>   no one who seeks God.

All have turned away,
   they have together become worthless;
there is no one who does good,
   not even one" (NIV).

Second, Paul looked at sin through the eyes of a physician:

"Their throats are open graves;
   their tongues practice deceit."
"The poison of vipers is on their lips."
   "Their mouths are full of cursing and bitterness"
      (Rom. 3:13-14, NIV).

Third, Paul looked at sin through the eyes of a historian:

"Their feet are swift to shed blood;
   ruin and misery mark their ways,
and the way of peace they do not know."
   "There is no fear of God before their eyes"
      (Rom. 3:15-18, NIV).

The proof of humankind's sin and lostness is evident not only in Scripture but also in observable human experience. For example:

According to the *Canadian Army Journal,* a former president of the Norwegian Academy of Sciences, aided by historians from England, Egypt, Germany, and India, came up with some fantastic figures and findings:
   Since 3600 B.C. the world has known only 292 years of peace. . . . There have been 14,531 wars, large and small, in which 3,640,000,000 people have been killed. The value of the destruction would pay for a gold belt around the world . . . 97.2 miles in width and . . . 33 feet thick.
   Since 650 B.C. there have been 1,656 arms races, only 16 of which have not ended in war. The remainder ended in the economic collapse of the countries concerned.[5]

Lost people act as they do because of their spiritual conditions. They are lost. It is amazing that human beings have made as much progress as they have, given their lost condition. Much good is in humankind. Yet wars, cruelty, human deprivation, and personal tragedy

12

stand as powerful evidence of the reality of human lostness. Even the best human beings experience emptiness and alienation from God. The tragedy of a life lived apart from God is the tragedy of personal lostness.

Jesus used the term *lost (apollumi)* a number of times. It has the strong meaning *to utterly destroy.* It is translated in various places as *to be ruined or rendered useless, to kill or destroy, to be wasted and useless,* and *to perish.*

In His three parables in Luke 15 Jesus described human lostness. He compared it to the lost sheep that has strayed and is in grave danger of destruction and ruin. The lost are like a lost coin that is useless, wasted, and worthless in its lostness. The lost are like the rebellious sons in the parable of the prodigal. One is lost in wasted living, away from the father in the far country of sin. The other is lost in an attitude of pride and self-centeredness. Lostness manifests itself in both acts and attitudes of life.

PERSONAL LEARNING ACTIVITY 3

The three parables in Luke 15 describe human lostness. Match each parable with the statement that best explains its meaning.

_____ 1. The parable of the lost sheep
_____ 2. The parable of the lost coin
_____ 3. The parable of the lost son
a. The lost are away from the father in a far country.
b. The lost are wasted in uselessness.
c. The lost are in grave danger of destruction and ruin.

The lost are spiritually dead (see Rom. 6:23; Eph. 2:1). A person has no power within to enliven himself. A man came to my office and said that he felt dead. He was alive physically, mentally, and emotionally, but at the very center of his being he was spiritually dead. He came to life that day as he received Jesus Christ, the only source of spiritual life.

The lost are objects of wrath (see Eph. 2:3). The lost abide under the wrath of God (see John 3:36). They live in unbelief, subject to the passions of a sinful nature, under the gloomy foreboding of impending judgment.

The lost are separated from Christ (see Eph. 2:12). They know no forgiveness. David cried out, "My sin is ever before me" (Ps. 51:3). Without forgiveness from the guilt of sin, stress and anxiety fill the hearts and minds of the lost. Often the lost may give the appearance of well-being. They may experience little or no concern about their relationships with God. Yet something is missing. Even if the outward appearance is one of success, confidence, and happiness, emptiness is at the core. This emptiness exists because humans are made for fellowship with God, and apart from Him they cannot experience completeness.

The lost are without God in the world (see Eph. 2:12). Although creations of God, they are not children of God. The lost have God's provision for life but not God's presence in life. They have received gifts but not the giver. They know about Him but do not know Him.

The most pitiful state of existence is to be without hope. The lost are without hope (see Eph. 2:12). No matter how difficult life becomes, people can go on if they see a ray of hope. The worst thing about hell is its hopelessness. The lost have no hope.

The lost are in sin (see John 8:24). They live in the realm of sin, "missing the mark" in their lives before God (see Rom. 3:23). They are enemies of Christ (see Matt. 12:30). There is no neutral position. Those who are not converted and committed to Him are against Him. They are children of the devil (see John 8:44). God is the Creator of every person but the Father only of those who have been born again by receiving Jesus Christ as Savior and Lord.

The lost are condemned already in unbelief (see John 3:18). It is not that they will be condemned when they die and stand before God in judgment. The sentence is already given. Judgment is settled. All that stands between the nonbeliever and eternal hell is one heartbeat.

The lost are spiritually blind (see 2 Cor. 4:3-4). The gospel is hidden to them. They are without understanding (see Rom. 3:11). They do not comprehend the things of God (see 1 Cor. 2:14). They grope through life like a blind person feeling for a wall. They stumble along the pathway of life in darkness.

The minds of the lost experience no peace, only continual turmoil:

> The wicked are like the tossing sea,
>> which cannot rest,
>> whose waves cast up mire and mud.
> "There is no peace," says my God, "for the wicked"
>> (Isa. 57:20-21, NIV).

The first time I saw the ceaseless, churning waves of the Pacific Ocean, my mind recalled these verses. The hearts of the lost endure the constant turmoil of restlessness.

The heartbreaking condition of the lost should arouse the church to urgency in taking the gospel of salvation to every person. Every Christian should be sensitive to the spiritual condition of every person and should seek an opportunity to share Christ with that person.

Lost in Sin: Consequences of Lostness

Human lostness is the most pathetic condition imaginable. The destiny of the lost has a twofold consequence: (1) It is the wasted existence of this present earthly life. (2) It is eternal separation from God in hell.

In this life. A lost person may achieve great accomplishments in society. His deeds may benefit humankind on this earth but be without eternal reward. The works that are done apart from the foundation of life in Christ will be burned as they are tried by fire (see 1 Cor. 3:11-15). Jesus told His disciples that only the fruit of life that abides in Him will remain: " 'Apart from me you can do nothing' " (John 15:5, NIV). Even "the plowing of the wicked, is sin" (Prov. 21:4). This verse and others suggest that all human activity is touched by the reality of sin. Even the good that people do is flawed and imperfect. Apart from God humans are incapable of good that is untouched by sin.

The condition of the lost is like the barren fig tree of Jesus' parable in Luke 13:6-9. The primary message of this parable is God's judgment on Israel, but this judgment also applies to a lost person who misses God's plan for his life. The owner of the vineyard plants, nurtures, and dresses the tree. He gives it time to bear fruit. It may provide shade. It may have beautiful foliage. But it does not fulfill the purpose of the owner. It bears no fruit! The decision of the owner is finally to cut it down: " 'Why should it use up the soil?' " (v. 7, NIV).

No fruit! Not fulfilling God's purpose for life is the heartbreaking result of a life of lostness.

In eternity. The destiny of the lost in eternity is an unparalleled tragedy. The lost are separated from God. The final consequence of Christ's rejection and lostness is eternal separation from God in hell. The doctrine of hell is the most terrible teaching in all the Scripture. It is a prominent word in the world's vocabulary. Yet there is a glaring silence on the subject in modern teaching and preaching in the church. Christians who deal with this awful subject have been accused of using "hellfire and brimstone" teachings and "scare tactics" to lead people to Christ. Also, it is true that some religionists have used the doctrine to reinforce a spirit of intimidation, condemnation, and judgmentalism.

The story has been told that an evangelist of the 19th century was seated with a group of Bible professors around a conference table. They were joking and enjoying fellowship when one of them told a light story about hell. Quickly the evangelist was on his feet and said, "Gentlemen, when you speak about hell, speak with tears in your voice."

Some of the finest advice I received as a young preacher was from a wise, older pastor as he spoke at a local pastors' conference. "Young men," he said, "when you preach on hell, don't do it as if you hope everybody is going there."

The doctrine of hell must not be ignored. When the biblical teaching about hell is ignored or treated lightly, evangelistic urgency is lost. People need to be saved *from* death and hell—as well as being saved *to* life and heaven.

Descriptive words. Several words are translated *hell* in our Bible. One is the word *hades*, which is the equivalent of the Old Testament Hebrew word *sheol*, meaning *the covered state*. It was the realm of the dead. Some Hebrews thought of *sheol* as divided into separate compartments for the righteous and the wicked. Paradise was thought of as the blissful abode of the righteous dead. There in the bosom of Abraham were joy and peace (see Luke 16:22).

Another word for hell is *tartarus*. Second Peter 2:4 speaks of the wicked angels imprisoned in *tartarus* in gloomy dungeons. *Tartarus* was the place in Greek thought where the wicked were punished deep in the bowels of the earth.

The Greek word *gehenna*, used 12 times in the New Testament, described the abode of the unrighteous dead. Deriving from a word that means *the valley of Hinnom*, it identifies a valley to the south of Jerusalem where the wicked kings Ahaz (see 2 Chron. 28:3) and Manasseh (see 2 Chron. 33:6) set up idols and caused the people to worship them. They led in the offering of human sacrifices and even offered their own children as sacrifices to the false gods.

Under good King Josiah's reforms the heathen idols and altars were destroyed. He made the valley *anathema,* a cursed place. It became the garbage dump of the city. Residents cast into the valley their garbage, bodies of dead animals, and bodies of the poor who died in the streets. A perpetual fire was kept burning. The maggots ate away at the dead bodies. Jesus speaks of *gehenna*, where the fire is not quenched and the worm does not die (see Mark 9:42-48).

Certainty of hell. Eternal hell is a certainty for those who die without Jesus Christ. Sensibility declares its certainty. In our system of finite justice we confine criminals, rapists, and murderers in prison. They cannot live freely among law-abiding citizens. Surely God, whose justice is infinite, will not allow the unrepentant, unregenerate into heaven. It is unthinkable that an unrepentant Adolf Hitler should walk the streets of gold with a redeemed John Wesley. If an unregenerate sinner were allowed into heaven, it would be unbearable to him. An unregenerate sinner could not stand in the presence of holy God.

Scripture declares the certainty of hell. In Matthew 5:22,29-30 in the Sermon on the Mount Jesus spoke strongly of a hell *(gehenna)* of fire. Matthew 7:13 speaks of the broad way that leads to destruction. Matthew 8:12; 22:13; 25:30 speak of outer darkness, where there are weeping and gnashing of teeth. Throughout the New Testament are declarations and warnings of the reality and danger of hell. It is worthy of notice that Jesus often spoke of hell and warned of its terrors.

In Luke 16:19-31 Jesus drew back the veil between the earthly and the eternal to permit us to see what hell is like. It is a place of suffering in eternal fire (see vv. 22-23). Some would interpret the fire as symbolic. My understanding is that the fire of hell is literal. But were it symbolic, the reality would be worse than the symbol.

Hell is a place of sorrow (see v. 25) and of mental and emotional anguish. "Son, remember" indicates that in hell memory is intensified. It is from the painful, agonizing memory of past sin and misspent lives that multitudes attempt to escape. But there is no escape. In hell awful memory tortures the mind and emotions.

Hell is a place of separation (see v. 26). There is no possibility for those in hell ever to escape. A great expanse is fixed so that those who would pass from hell to heaven cannot.

The worst fact about hell is its hopelessness. If one could go to hell and hope to escape one day, it would not be hell. Hell is conclusive. It is eternal. Hell is a place of unending, unbearable, yet inescapable suffering and sorrow. At the end of the age death and hell will be cast into the lake of fire forever with the devil and his angels (see Rev. 20:14).

PERSONAL LEARNING ACTIVITY 4

Review the first paragraph in "Lost in Sin: Consequences of Lostness" and complete the following statement by filling in the appropriate words.

The destiny of the lost has a twofold consequence: (1) It is the
_____ _____ of this present earthly life. (2) It
is _____   _____ from   God   in
_____.

Conclusion

The study of salvation begins with an understanding of biblical teachings about human lostness. The lost have lost their lives on earth.
They will be lost forever in eternal hell. A barrier of sin stands between God and all humankind. All have sinned personally and come
short of the glory of God (see Rom. 3:23). Humans in their sin are
without excuse (see Rom. 1:18-20). "The wages of sin is death" (spiritual separation from God, Rom. 6:23, NIV). Jesus said, " 'Unless you
repent, you too will all perish' " (Luke 13:3, NIV). The heartrending
condition of all humankind is separation from God and spiritual
death. Eternal separation in hell is one heartbeat away. Except for
God's gracious provision of salvation in and through Jesus Christ,
every person would be eternally lost.

We now turn to God's eternal plan to redeem lost humankind.

DOCTRINE IN LIFE

On the lines below list three or more persons who you believe
are lost. Begin today to pray at least once each day for these
persons for at least one week.

1. _____

2. _____

3. _____

4. _____

5. _____

---

[1]Scripture quotations marked NIV are from the Holy Bible, *New International Version*,
copyright © 1973, 1978, 1984 by International Bible Society.
[2]Shirley C. Guthrie, Jr., *Christian Doctrine* (Richmond: The Covenant Life Curriculum

Press, 1968), 217-18.
[3]Bert Dominy, *God's Work of Salvation, Layman's Library of Christian Doctrine* (Nashville: Broadman Press, 1986), 24.
[4]Herschel H. Hobbs, *Romans* (Waco: Word Books, 1977), 42-43.
[5]Paul Lee Tan, *Encyclopedia of 7,700 Illustrations: Signs of the Times* (Rockville: Assurance Publishers, 1979), 1571.

God's Eternal Plan

QUESTIONS TO GUIDE YOUR STUDY
1. What does it mean to say that salvation is God's eternal plan?
2. How has God taken the initiative in human salvation?
3. How does God's call of Israel relate to His saving purpose?
4. How did the Old Testament prophets prepare God's people for the coming of Christ?

This study of the doctrine of salvation is not a study of some clever scheme of humankind. Nor does this study relate to vague ideas about the purposes of God. The study of the doctrine of salvation is a study of God on mission. Salvation is the theme of the entire Bible because salvation is at the heart of everything God has chosen to reveal to us about Himself.

In *The Biblical Basis of Missions* Avery T. Willis, Jr., wrote: "Missions originated in the heart of God. It is not something we decide to do for God, but God reveals his purpose to us so that we may have a creative part in his mission. Make no mistake, we do not initiate the mission nor will we consummate it."[1]

Our study will take us to the very heart of God. It will focus on His eternal purpose of redemption. This redeeming purpose weaves its way through the entire Bible and finds its ultimate fulfillment in Jesus Christ. Paul summed up God's all-encompassing redemptive purpose: "Now in Christ Jesus you who once were far away have been brought near through the blood of Christ" (Eph. 2:13, NIV).

Salvation: Based on God's Initiative

Salvation is not an afterthought with God. The pitiful scene of a guilty Adam in the garden of Eden did not take God by surprise. God's plan of salvation is not a patchwork attempt to salvage a spoiled creation.

The doctrine of salvation is rooted in God's eternal purpose. It is centered in Christ. Before the world was, Jesus was "the Lamb slain from the foundation of the world" (Rev. 13:8). When Jesus stepped into human history, John identified Him as "the Lamb of God, which taketh away the sin of the world" (John 1:29).

God on the throne of His sovereignty is working out His eternal purpose of redemption. The apostle Peter wrote:

> Forasmuch as ye know that ye were not redeemed with corruptible things, as silver and gold, from your vain conversation received by tradition from your fathers; but with the precious blood of Christ, as of a lamb without blemish and without spot: who verily was foreordained before the foundation of the world, but was manifest in these last times for you, who by him do believe in God, that raised him up from the dead, and gave him glory; that your faith and hope might be in God (1 Pet. 1:18-21).

God purposed redemption in Christ for humans before creation took place (see Eph. 1:3-14). Based on His sovereign foreknowledge and on His provision for human free will, God predestined those who would be in Christ to be conformed to the likeness of His Son. Romans 8:30 indicates that those He predestined, He also called; those He called, He also justified; those He justified, He also glorified.

Thus, when we address the subject of salvation, we address that which is at the heart of God's character and purpose. Salvation—in its design, fulfillment, and consummation—is God's initiative.

PERSONAL LEARNING ACTIVITY 5

Write one sentence to explain what you believe the author meant when he wrote that salvation is not an afterthought with God.

_____

_____

_____

Salvation: The Central Purpose of Creation

Salvation is the central purpose of creation. The motif of redemption is seen in the earliest record of God's creative plan. From the beginning God determined to redeem the persons He had created. Although the coming of Christ into the world was many centuries away, God laid the foundation for salvation in His earliest dealings with humankind. The Creator would also be the Savior.

The creative power. The opening words of the Bible are "In the beginning God" (Gen. 1:1). God is preexistent and self-existent. The Hebrew word for *God* in Genesis 1:1 is *Elohim. El* means *mighty One* or *the Almighty.* The word ending is plural, indicating not that there are plural gods but that the one God is three persons.[2] He is a triune God. God is Father, Son, and Holy Spirit. Genesis 1:1 foreshadows the Trinity revealed by God through the unfolding of His revelation in His Word.

The activity of the triune God is seen in Genesis 1—2. In the beginning God created. The Spirit hovered over the waters when the earth was formless and empty, and darkness was over the surface of the deep. God spoke and said, " 'Let there be . . .' " (Gen. 1:3), and there was!

Christ is the agency of all creation. As the eternal Word, He was with God in the beginning. In fact, He is God: "In the beginning was the Word, and the Word was with God, and the Word was God. He was with God in the beginning. Through him all things were made; without him nothing was made that has been made" (John 1:1-3, NIV). "The Word became flesh and made his dwelling among us. We have seen his glory, the glory of the One and Only, who came from the Father, full of grace and truth" (John 1:14, NIV).

Paul elaborated further on the supremacy of Christ: "By him all things were created: things in heaven and on earth" (Col. 1:16, NIV). Before the beginning, when the material universe did not yet exist, God—Father, Son, and Holy Spirit—existed in perfect love and communication. Ultimate reality existed apart from the material universe and apart from humans. The personal God, the Trinity, lived face-to-face with Himself in love and communication. God did not create from a deficiency, a need to have an object for His love. God's self-sufficiency is absolute. The mystery of creation is that as an act of His free will, He chose to create everything. Although this defies human understanding, it is revealed by God Himself.

The creative purpose. From His eternal and changeless nature God created everything that exists. Creation was the purposeful act of

22

God, not a mere accident resulting from a haphazard combination of elements. The world exists because God willed it to be. A recurring theme in the Bible is creation by the word of God. Ten times in Genesis 1 the phrase "God said" occurs (see vv. 3,6,9,11,14,20,24,26,28-29). The psalmist praised God thus:

> By the word of the Lord were the heavens made,
>> their starry host by the breath of his mouth.
> For he spoke, and it came to be;
>> he commanded, and it stood firm" (Ps. 33:6,9, NIV).

Bert Dominy has meaningfully interpreted the word *created* in Genesis 1:1 as follows: "The verb 'create' *(bara)* is special in the Old Testament. It always has God as its subject; it is never used of human activity. . . . The verb implies that God created the world 'out of nothing' *(ex nihilo)*. God's creativity is unique. Creation, therefore, has a quality that is different from anything made by human hands."[3] Of this uniqueness the writer of Hebrews declared, "By faith we understand that the universe was formed by God's command, so that what is seen was not made out of what was visible" (Heb. 11:3, NIV).

The universe God created was good. The proclamation "God saw that it was good" is repeated throughout the creation account (see Gen. 1). There is nothing inherently evil in the material world. The world is good because it was created and declared good by the good God.

The creation of persons. The creation account places special emphasis on the creation of persons. Material or biological forces cannot account for persons. God made persons in His own image as a special act independent from the creation of the lower forms of animal life. He created humans to have dominion over all the other creatures He had made.

In a picturesque fashion the account of the creation of persons is given. "God said, 'Let us make man in our image, in our likeness, and let them rule . . .' " (Gen. 1:26, NIV). Here God—Father, Son, and Holy Spirit—in love and communication expresses His sovereignty to create persons not as gods but in His image. Although they are not divine, they are sacred. They are not part of God but are made in His image and likeness. God created Adam from the dust of the ground, shaping his body from the elements of the earth. Paul declared that persons are of the earth and are earthy. Adam was a lifeless form until God "breathed into his nostrils the breath of life, and the man became a living being [soul]" (Gen. 2:7, NIV).

Persons were created in the image of God to live in fellowship with God, and God declared His creative act good. God provided perfectly for every need of the persons He had created. God placed them in a perfect home, the garden of Eden. God gave them perfect employment, to work in the garden and to take care of it (see Gen. 2:15). Work is not a judgment for sin. God's assignment of work predated sin. Work is a part of God's purpose for persons.

The first occasion on which God said, "It is not good" is in Genesis 2:18: " 'It is not good for the man to be alone. I will make a helper suitable for him' " (NIV). God caused a deep sleep to fall on Adam. He took one of his ribs and from it made a woman and brought her to the man. Adam broke forth in praise for God's gift:

> "This is now bone of my bones
> and flesh of my flesh;
> she shall be called 'woman,'
> for she was taken out of man."

For this reason a man will leave his father and mother and be united to his wife, and they will become one flesh. The man and his wife were both naked, and they felt no shame (Gen. 2:23-25, NIV).

These verses reveal God's intention for marriage: the man and the woman living in unbroken fellowship with Him and with each other. The key to harmony and joy in the home is one man and one woman in fellowship with God, living in love and communication with each other and with Him.

What does the expression *image and likeness of God* mean? The nature of persons is both material and immaterial. The material is the human body. The immaterial (soul) is described by such terms as *intellect, mind, heart, conscience, soul,* and *spirit.* "Man is twofold in nature. He is both spirit and body. Man is not a body and has a soul. He is a soul and has a body. The body is mortal; the soul is immortal."[4] God is Spirit. The term *image and likeness of God* indicates that man is a spiritual personality with a capacity for God.

W. T. Conner has listed four essential functions or powers that belong to human beings as spiritual personalities made in the image and likeness of God:

First is intelligence, or the power to think. Human beings are distinct from lower animals. They have the power to know themselves and to know God. Self-consciousness is one mark of personality. It is the power to know self as related to other things and persons.

Second is the power of rational affection. The lower animals have sensibility and instinctive affection. But human beings have the capacity for rational love, the ability to give themselves deliberately and sacrificially for the good of the ones who are loved. This is not blind sentiment, instinct, or mere passion. It is the capacity for love like God's love.

Third is free will. Persons are free beings with the power of self-determination. They can be influenced but not forced. They have the capacity for choice. They do what they will to do. Their freedom is limited but real. They have the power to establish ideals and plans and to move toward those ideals.

Fourth, persons are like God in possessing a moral sense. They have a conscience, an innate sense of right and wrong. One's moral sense may be dulled or misdirected; nonetheless, he has a consciousness that either approves or disapproves of his attitudes and acts.[5]

God created persons for fellowship with Himself. Persons have a capacity for knowing God and for fellowship with Him in love, a spiritual affinity for God. In their original state of innocence human beings knew God and loved Him. They have an insatiable thirst for fellowship with Him. It has been said that every person is born on a quest for God. There can be no rest until rest is found in God.

The choice to disobey. Love is the nature of God: "God is love" (1 John 4:16). God loves every person (see John 3:16). Love desires love in return; but love, to be real, cannot be manipulated or forced. It must be freely bestowed. Persons could not be puppets on a string, manipulated into loving God, if the love relationship were to be genuine. If we resembled robots with programmed responses, we could not know and respond to God's pure and perfect love. Therefore, God made persons free. He has given every person free will. Each person is free to choose God or to reject Him. Each person has the freedom of will to love God and live in fellowship with Him or to rebel against Him.

Without opportunity for choice there can be no actual freedom of will. If only good exists, with no possibility for evil, then there can be no choice or free exercise of the will. Thus, God acted to establish the possibility for persons to choose between good and evil.

Genesis 2:15-17 records the circumstance that provided human beings an opportunity to exercise freedom of will. In the garden God provided for all of their needs. He planted fruit trees that were pleasing to the eye and good for food. In the middle of the garden were the tree of life and the tree of the knowledge of good and evil (see Gen. 2:9). God gave Adam one command: " 'You are free to eat from any tree in the garden; but you must not eat from the tree of the knowledge of good and evil, for when you eat of it you will surely die' " (Gen. 2:16-17, NIV).

Now human beings had an opportunity to know good from evil by choosing good and rejecting evil or by choosing evil and rejecting good. They could exercise free will by obeying or disobeying God's one command.

The inspired record of the fall and its devastating consequences is in Genesis 3. Here the tempter entered the picture, appearing as a serpent. Before the fall the serpent must have been attractive and graceful. Paul said that Satan appears as an angel of light (see 2 Cor. 11:14). Genesis 3:1 says that the serpent is more crafty (subtle) than any of the animals.

Questioning God's goodness and integrity was the tempter's approach to Eve. Satan suggested to her that God was withholding a good thing from her and Adam: " 'Did God really say, "You must not eat from any tree in the garden"?' " He first used the subtle power of insinuation to accuse God and to appeal to the woman's curiosity. The woman answered the serpent, " 'We may eat fruit from the trees in the garden, but God did say, "You must not eat fruit from the tree that is in the middle of the garden, and you must not touch it, or you will die" ' " (Gen. 3:1-3, NIV). God had not said, "You must not touch it." This was added by the woman, perhaps revealing a growing resentment toward the command. Thus, Eve entertained the temptation by listening further to Satan. Then Satan, the accuser and slanderer, directly charged God: " 'You will not surely die. . . . For God knows that when you eat of it your eyes will be opened, and you will be like God, knowing good and evil' " (vv. 4-5, NIV).

Satan ignored the fact that God had bountifully provided their needs. He deceitfully focused on one command, distorting the fact that this prohibition was for their benefit. He planted the seed of doubt, as if to say, "What was God's real reason for giving you this command?"

The temptation was an appeal to basic, God-given needs, desires, and drives. Sin resulted when the man and the woman attempted to satisfy God-given desires in a God-forbidden way. Satan cannot be charged with the blame for their sin. "The devil made me do it" is an empty attempt to avoid responsibility. A person is responsible for his or her own sin. The devil has the power only to "put out the bait," like a fisher baiting a hook to catch a fish. The fish takes the bait. "One is tempted when, by his own evil desire, he is dragged away and enticed. Then, after desire has conceived, it gives birth to sin, and sin, when it is full-grown, gives birth to death" (Jas. 1:14-15, NIV).

A threefold temptation enticed Eve. When Eve "saw that the fruit of the tree was good for food and pleasing to the eye, and also desirable for gaining wisdom, she took some and ate it" (Gen. 3:6, NIV). The temptation appealed to God-given desires or drives for food, beauty, and wisdom. Satan appealed to the physical, sensual appetite; to the aesthetic desire for beauty; and to pride, the desire to be the god of one's own life. Satan still levels the same temptation at human beings through "the lust of the flesh, and the lust of the eyes, and the pride of life" (1 John 2:16).

Eve took some of the fruit and ate and gave some to her husband, who also ate. Adam and Eve had sinned, thus introducing sin into the world. Sin is rebellion against the will of God. It is seen in the Bible as missing the mark, crookedness, lawlessness, iniquity, wickedness, offense, and unbelief. The basis of all sin is self-centeredness rather than God-centeredness. Any transgression of God's will is sin (see Jas. 2:9-11).

The initiative of God. The result of sin was immediate. The couple's eyes were opened. Seeing that they were naked, they sewed together fig leaves, attempting to cover themselves and the shame of their sin. When they heard the Lord God in the garden, they ran and hid themselves. Adam and Eve should have run through the garden seeking God and crying, "O God, we have sinned!" The pattern of sin was set to continue through the stream of human history. Paul quoted Psalm 14:2-3 to describe the guilt response of humankind:

"There is no one who understands,
no one who seeks God.
All have turned away,
they have together become worthless"
(Rom. 3:11-12, NIV).

It was God who took the initiative to seek out the sinners in the garden. Before confronting them with their sin, God pronounced judgment on the serpent. The serpent was sentenced to crawl on its belly and to eat dust all the days of its life (see Gen. 3:14). From His great compassion and mercy God gave a promise of deliverance. Then from His holiness He brought judgment on human sin:

> "I will put enmity
>   between you and the woman,
>   and between your offspring and hers;
> he will crush your head,
>   and you will strike his heel" (Gen. 3:15, NIV).

Many feel that the virgin birth is implied in God's promise that the offspring (singular) of woman (not man) will crush the head of the serpent. In His death for sin and in His resurrection Jesus dealt the death blow to the head of the serpent. The serpent bruised Jesus' heel at the cross when Jesus died.

God then dealt with man and woman about their sin. Man's work would become painful toil, with a sin-cursed earth that would produce "thorns and thistles." Man would be engaged in a perpetual struggle against nature. Woman's childbearing would be painful (see Gen. 3:16-19).

Adam and Eve were naked, guilty, and ashamed. In tender mercy God made garments of skin to clothe them. Many see in this act the first indication of the shedding of the blood of the innocent to cover the guilty. The blood of innocent animals was shed to provide a covering for guilty sinners, pointing to the shedding of the righteous blood of the Son of God as a propitiation for, or covering of, human sin (see 1 John 2:2).

The final consequence of sin was the banishment of man and woman from the garden so they would not eat of the tree of life and live forever in their sinful state. Although this was an act of judgment against sin, it was also an act of mercy. In choosing sin, humans had died spiritually. To live forever in physical existence would be an intolerable tragedy. God intervened with loving-kindness to allow them to die physically.

From the beginning in the garden of Eden all of human history unfolded God's plan of redemption, which climaxed in the coming of Christ as the Lamb of God, slain before the foundation of the world. The holiness of God was manifested as He intervened in a twofold confrontation of sin. First, His holiness was seen through His justice in demanding a penalty for sin. The penalty for sin is death (see Rom. 6:23). Second, His holiness was manifested through His love in providing salvation. God provided for the payment of the penalty of sin through the death and resurrection of His Son (see 2 Cor. 5:21).

P E R S O N A L   L E A R N I N G   A C T I V I T Y   6

The Bible teaches that humans are made in the image of God. Choose the statement that you believe *best* explains what this means.

_____ 1. We have a physical appearance like God's.
_____ 2. Humans are creative like the Creator.
_____ 3. Humans have been given the spiritual capacity for a relationship and fellowship with God.

Salvation: The Focal Point of Scripture

The story of redemption flows through the Bible like a mighty river. The Old Testament is God's self-revelation of His working in the world and in and through His chosen people, Israel, to point to and prepare for Christ's coming. The New Testament is God's revelation of Himself in Christ, reconciling the world to Himself.

Through the lives of individuals, the history of Israel, and the prophets, God revealed a principle in the Old Testament that is fully developed in the New Testament: Sacrifice is necessary if sin is to be forgiven. God's initiative in providing for humankind's salvation through an adequate atonement for sin is grace. Humankind's response in believing God and accepting Christ and His atonement is faith. Grace and faith are the two sides of the coin of salvation.

God's dealing with individuals. God began to move through history to reveal His salvation to humankind. The biblical record focuses on some individuals with whom God dealt in specifically redemptive ways.

Abel. The first glimpse of forgiveness by faith through the shedding of blood was Abel's sacrifice of the firstborn of the flock. Cain, his brother, chose to bring an offering of the fruit of his fields to God. The Bible relates that God accepted Abel's offering but was not pleased with Cain's offering.

Why did Abel's offering please God? The reason given in the New Testament is: "By faith Abel offered God a better sacrifice than Cain did" (Heb. 11:4). Many believe that his blood offering was accepted because it prefigures the death of Christ for sin and illustrates the truth that runs throughout the Bible that sin requires sacrifice, the shedding of blood (see Heb. 9:22).

Noah. God continued to reveal His purpose of salvation through Noah and his deliverance from the flood. When human wickedness was great and violence filled the earth, God determined to destroy the world with a flood of water (see Gen. 6). But "Noah found grace in the eyes of the Lord" (Gen. 6:8). Noah believed God and built an ark, and he and his family were saved. Noah's first act after stepping from the ark was to build an altar and to offer a sacrifice to God. By grace through faith humanity was preserved to begin anew. Noah's sacrifice expressed his faith in and gratitude toward God for His deliverance.

Abraham. As the human family multiplied and spread throughout the earth, God chose and called Abram, through whom He would reveal Himself and His redemptive plan to the world. God spoke to Abram in the land of Ur and called him to go to a land that God would show him. Abram, later known as Abraham, responded by faith and went, not knowing where he would go—only that God would show him (see Gen. 12:1). God covenanted with Abraham that He would make of him a great nation, that He would bless him and make his name great. As a result, Abraham would be a blessing. God would bless those who blessed Abraham and curse those who cursed him, and through him all the peoples of the earth would be blessed (see Gen. 12:2-3).

God chose Abraham, one man who "believed God, and it was counted unto him for righteousness" (Rom. 4:3). From that one man God shaped a nation, through whom He would reveal Himself and His salvation to all nations. Abraham and Sarah were childless. But God promised a descendant. When Abraham was 99 and Sarah was 90, God gave them Isaac, a miracle son.

Slowly but certainly, God developed a nation for His purpose. God promised to give Abraham the land of Canaan. Many years would pass before this promise would be a reality. God told Abraham that for four hundred years his descendants would be strangers in another country, where they would be enslaved and mistreated but afterward would come out with great possessions (see Gen. 15:12-16).

Moses. Through Abraham God moved to raise up a family—Isaac, Jacob, and the 12 sons of Jacob. Joseph, one of Jacob's sons, was sold into slavery by his jealous brothers. God honored Joseph's faithfulness and caused him to become a great man in Egypt. The Israelites multiplied and prospered in Egypt. Then a Pharaoh came to power in Egypt who did not know about Joseph's accomplishments or care about his descendants. By this time the Israelites had become so numerous in Egypt that they were perceived as a threat to Pharaoh. Pharaoh hated the Israelites and determined to crush them in cruel slavery. As slaves in Egypt, the Israelites cried to God for deliverance. With a mighty hand God raised up Moses and sent 10 dreadful plagues to break the back of Egyptian power and to deliver His people Israel. The final plague was that of death of the firstborn of every Egyptian family. Each family of the Israelites was instructed to kill a sacrificial lamb and to place its blood on the door frames of the dwelling. The Israelites were to roast the lamb and eat it, along with unleavened bread (the bread of haste) and bitter herbs (symbolizing the bitterness of their bondage). God promised that the death angel would pass over the houses that were marked with blood (see Ex. 12:13). The firstborn of that home would be saved from death.

As God had promised Abraham (see Gen. 15:14), the Egyptians handed over their treasures to the Israelites and urged them to leave Egypt. Under the leadership of Moses, God delivered Israel, divided the Red Sea, brought them to safety on the other side, and destroyed the enemy's army.

God instructed Israel to celebrate the Passover annually to commemorate its glorious deliverance from Egypt. The Passover pointed to the reality of persons' deliverance from the slavery of sin, which would be accomplished in the death and resurrection of Christ. The shed blood of the lamb of the first year, without spot or blemish, typified the shedding of Jesus' sinless blood to deliver all persons from the slavery of sin.

God instituted the Passover feast so that the people of Israel would never forget how God had delivered them from their bondage. Centuries later, Christ came and gave His life on the cross. As the shedding of the blood of the Passover lamb symbolized God's deliverance of His people, so the shedding of Christ's blood on the cross provides redemption and deliverance to all who believe in Jesus. Paul interpreted the Passover in 1 Corinthians 5:7: "Christ, our Passover lamb, has been sacrificed" (NIV). In the Passover God was instructing and preparing a people through whom He would send His Son to be Savior.

PERSONAL LEARNING ACTIVITY 7

On the lines below write a sentence that explains what you believe Paul meant when he referred to Christ as "our Passover lamb."

God's purpose in Israel. God's revelation of His purpose and plan of salvation and His preparation of Israel continued as He led the Israelites into the wilderness. They camped at the foot of Mount Sinai. Moses went up into the mountain, where he received the law from God. The law was given as "our schoolmaster to bring us unto Christ, that we might be justified by faith" (Gal. 3:24). God designed it to confront persons with their need of a Savior and to lead them to Christ.

The law has been divided into three general divisions: "(1) The Moral Law which is briefly stated in the Ten Commandments. (2) The Ceremonial Law containing all the details of worship, such as sacrifices, the priesthood, holy seasons, and many other such matters. Every phase of the religious life of this new nation whose unique mission was a religious one, was provided for in these detailed instructions. (3) The Judicial part had to do with civil law."[6] These guided the Israelites in their everyday interactions and relationships, such as buying and selling property, administering justice, and court procedures. When Moses presented God's law to the people of Israel, they accepted it and entered a covenant relationship with Yahweh, the eternal God who had saved them and who had created a nation from slaves (see Ex. 24:1-8).

Christ was revealed as the fulfillment of the law (see Matt. 5:17). He lived the moral law to the fullest. In fulfilling it, He filled it full of the meaning God intended. He made it clear that keeping the law concerns the attitude of the heart as well as the act.

Christ also fulfilled the ceremonial law. The Book of Hebrews presents Christ as the fulfillment of the Old Testament sacrifices, offerings, feasts, and priesthood. When Jesus died, rose again, and ascended to take His place at the right hand of God to give access to all who would come to God through Him, He fulfilled the ceremonial law. Christ is the reality toward whom the ceremonies of the law pointed.

God's message through the prophets. God continued His work in the life of Israel to prepare for the coming of His Son. In the wilderness

He molded the Israelites into a nation through the leadership of Moses. Then God appointed Joshua, whose name is the Old Testament equivalent of *Jesus,* to lead the Israelites to cross the Jordan and to conquer the promised land. During the hundreds of years between the settlement of Israel in Canaan and the birth of Jesus, God raised up prophets. Intermittently, these anointed representatives of God brought prophetic messages that pointed to God's redemptive purpose, which would be perfectly revealed in Christ.

Generally, God used prophets to remind Israel of its mission as a nation of priests and to call the people of God to repentance and true worship of God. Specifically, through the prophets He gave definite promises for the coming of Christ, the Messiah. These have been termed messianic promises.

Even before the period of the prophets in Israel's history, God gave His word of promise about Christ. He is the seed of woman who will bruise the head of the serpent (see Gen. 3:15). He is the promised seed of Abraham (see Gen. 12:3; 18:18). He is the promised seed of Isaac (see Gen. 17:19). Christ is the "star out of Jacob" and the "scepter out of Israel" (Num. 24:17, NIV). Jacob prophesied that He would descend from the tribe of Judah (see Gen. 49:10). Moses predicted that God would raise up a prophet like himself to whom they should listen (see Deut. 18:15). David spoke of His sufferings in Psalm 22.

During the period of the prophets, God prepared His people through prophecies of facts and events about the Messiah. Isaiah gave numerous messianic promises and prophecies. The Christ would be the heir to the throne of David (see Isa. 9:7). He would be born of a virgin (see Isa. 7:14). The Spirit of the Lord—of wisdom, understanding, counsel, and might—would be upon Him (see Isa. 11:2). He would suffer vicariously like a lamb led to the slaughter (see Isa. 53:6-7). He would be silent when accused (see Isa. 53:7). He would be put to death with sinners (see Isa. 53:12). He would be our sin bearer (see Isa. 53:4-5). Micah prophesied that He would be born in Bethlehem (see Mic. 5:2). Hosea predicted His flight into Egypt (see Hos.11:1). Jeremiah predicted the massacre of the infants after His birth (see Jer. 31:15). Zechariah prophesied His triumphal entry (see Zech. 9:9).

The Prophets and Psalms give numerous other prophecies. Jesus and the New Testament writers declare many of these prophecies fulfilled in specific events of Jesus' life. God's purpose was to provide salvation so that persons could live with Him in the fellowship of His love and have communication with Him, as illustrated throughout the pages of the Old Testament.

During the period of the prophets in 722 B.C. the Northern Kingdom of Israel fell to the Assyrians, and the people of the Northern Kingdom were dispersed among the nations. In 587 B.C. the Southern Kingdom of Judah was taken into captivity to Babylon. A remnant of Judah returned to rebuild the city of Jerusalem and the temple.

Preparation for the Savior. The Old Testament Scriptures came to a close with the prophecy of Malachi. A four-hundred-year period of prophetic silence followed, often referred to as the interbiblical period. Although no new word from God came through the prophets, God's unseen hand continued to move in the affairs of nations and individuals.

Several institutions and movements began during the Babylonian captivity and the interbiblical period that prepared the world for Christ's coming and for the spread of the gospel. The development of the synagogue during the Babylonian captivity gave rise to the establishment of local meeting places for worship and religious instruction in Jewish communities, wherever they had been scattered. The synagogues were natural places for the disciples to begin preaching and teaching the gospel of Christ. They first went to the synagogues to announce that Christ, the Messiah, had come. Synagogues provided a pattern or form for local churches during the apostolic period.

The providence of God was setting the scene for the coming of His Son. The rise to power of the Greek Empire under Alexander the Great resulted in a universal language. The preciseness of the Greek language allowed the possibility for communicating the gospel meaningfully throughout the known world.

Rome was the dominant world power when Jesus was born. The Greek Empire had fallen to mighty Rome. Rome placed the world of Jesus' day under one government. It developed roads and travel routes, enhancing the possibility of travel with relative safety from country to country. Rome developed a postal system, which made possible more efficient and effective communication through writing. The apostle Paul took full advantage of this means by writing epistles, or letters.

The spiritual climate among the Jews created an atmosphere of expectancy that the hope of God's people, the coming of the Messiah, was near. The time was right! The sovereign God had prepared the scene of history for His intervention in the human situation to reveal His love and to provide salvation: "When the time had fully come, God sent His Son, born of a woman, born under law, to redeem those under the law, that we might receive the full rights of sons" (Gal. 4:4-

5, NIV). "The Word became flesh and made His dwelling among us" (John 1:14, NIV). God's eternal plan was revealed in history.

DOCTRINE IN LIFE

This chapter has emphasized salvation as the plan of God from eternity. To accomplish this plan, God worked in many ways through many persons. God also works in many ways through many persons to bring salvation to individuals. Make a list of the persons whom God used in a special way to bring you to your salvation experience. You may list one person or several.

1. _____

2. _____

3. _____

4. _____

5. _____

6. _____

Reflect on the persons whose names you have listed and take the following actions this week.

1. Thank God for each person who helped you come to Christ.
2. Contact each person on the list who is still living, if you know how to find that person. You may do this by a personal visit, a card, a letter, or a telephone call. Express appreciation for the person's role in leading you to salvation.

---

[1]Avery T. Willis, Jr., *The Biblical Basis of Missions* (Nashville: Convention Press, 1984), 23.

[2]Robert L. Hamblin and William H. Stephens, *The Doctrine of Lordship* (Nashville: Convention Press, 1990), 23.

[3]Bert Dominy, *God's Work of Salvation, Layman's Library of Christian Doctrine* (Nashville: Broadman Press, 1986), 13.

[4]Herschel H. Hobbs, *The Baptist Faith and Message* (Nashville: Convention Press, 1971), 51.

[5]W. T. Conner, *Revelation and God* (Nashville: Broadman Press, 1936), 50-52.

[6]H. I. Hester, *The Heart of Hebrew History* (Liberty: The Quality Press, Inc., 1962), 125.

Responding to God's Plan

QUESTIONS TO GUIDE YOUR STUDY
1. *Why are decisions in life so important?*
2. *Why does a person have to repent to be saved?*
3. *What does it mean to have faith in Jesus?*
4. *What does baptism symbolize? Why is it important?*
5. *At what age can a child be saved?*

Decisions! Decisions! Decisions! Life is filled with demands for decisions. Some are seemingly insignificant, made in the course of everyday life. What clothes shall I wear today? What breakfast food shall I eat this morning? Others affect all of life. What profession or job shall I pursue? What school would best prepare me for my life's work? Whom shall I marry?

Very few things happen in anybody's life that do not involve responses and decisions. Each person is who and what he is because of these responses and decisions. In the course of each person's life many decisions must be made. The greatest decision every person faces is reflected in the question of Pontius Pilate to the multitude in Jerusalem after he had interrogated Jesus and had Him beaten. Torn with the conflict of emotion between right and expediency, he addressed the crowd: "What shall I do then with Jesus which is called Christ?" (Matt. 27:22).

Pilate's experience is the experience of every person. God requires a response to Jesus Christ. Paul stood on Mars Hill and declared to the intellectual Athenians that God " 'commands all people everywhere to repent. For he has set a day when he will judge the world with justice by the man he has appointed. He has given proof of this to all men by raising him from the dead' " (Acts 17:30-31, NIV). Every person must decide whether to repent, accept Jesus Christ, and follow

RESPONDING TO GOD'S PLAN

Him or to reject and deny Him.

The response one makes to Jesus Christ involves the totality of life: emotion (feeling), intellect (rational mind), will (personal, inner determination), and life-style (following Christ in daily living). The decision to accept Jesus Christ and to experience salvation is based on two realities. The first is God's initiative, what God has done to provide salvation and to reveal that provision to humanity. The second is human responsibility, what a person must do in response to God's provision and revelation.

Salvation: The Divine Provision

Humankind is incurably religious. In every person is a God-shaped void. People seek to fill that void and to reach God through their own achievements. People have devised ingenious methods and systems in attempting to achieve right relationships with God. But they always fall short (see Rom. 3:23). God spoke through Isaiah:

> "As the heavens are higher than the earth,
>   so are my ways higher than your ways
> and my thoughts than your thoughts"
>   (Isa. 55:9, NIV).

The religions of the world represent futile human attempts to reach God. Christianity is God's initiative through Christ to reach all people.

A response to Jesus Christ that results in salvation is based on God's provision for humankind's redemption and forgiveness of sin through the cross and the resurrection of His Son. Through Christ's coming in human flesh, living a sinless life, satisfying the demands of the law, dying a sacrificial death for sin, and rising from the dead to conquer sin and death, God intervened in the human situation to provide eternal salvation.

The human situation was hopeless (see Eph. 2:12). All people were hopelessly separated from God (see Rom. 6:23). All were under sin, with an impenetrable sin barrier between themselves and God (see Rom. 3:9). Through self-effort humans could never break through the barrier of sin and present themselves in righteousness to God. Humans could not transact their own salvation. A divine transaction was necessary. God acted in Christ to do what people could not do. He penetrated the sin barrier to provide the way for people to come to Him through Christ.

37

At the cross God dealt with sin through a miraculous work. From the depth of His agony on the cross, Jesus cried to the Father, " 'My God, my God, why have you forsaken me?' " (Matt. 27:46, NIV). On the cross "God made him who had no sin to be sin for us, so that in him we might become the righteousness of God" (2 Cor. 5:21, NIV). Bible students have grappled with the meaning of such passages. We know that Jesus was completely sinless. He had never known the haunting guilt and hollow emptiness of sin. But suddenly on the cross He felt the combined intensity of all the guilt for all humankind's sin of all time. Throughout eternity His fellowship with the Father had never been broken. He was one with the Father. But at the cross Jesus became sin for us: "He himself bore our sins in his body on the tree, so that we might die to sins and live for righteousness; by his wounds you have been healed" (1 Pet. 2:24, NIV). Sin did its worst. It killed the sinless Son of God. Satan had bruised the heel of the seed of woman (see Gen. 3:15).

Immediately before He died on Calvary, Jesus said, "It is finished" (John 19:30). This was not the final sigh of a dying man, indicating that His suffering was over. It was a shout of triumph. It was a mission accomplished! That for which Jesus came had been done. Once for all, the sin debt was paid. He had broken through the sin barrier to provide the way for whoever will come to God through Him.

An amazing and highly significant thing happened as Jesus died on the cross. We are told by the Gospel writers that the veil in the temple in Jerusalem was torn from top to bottom (see Matt. 27:51; Mark 15:38; Luke 23:45). The curtain separated Jewish worshipers from the holy of holies. Only the high priest could go behind that curtain, and he could go only once a year to offer a sacrifice for the sins of the people. That curtain was a constant reminder of a grim reality: Sinful human beings did not have direct access to the holy God. Sin had created a barrier that human beings could not overcome. When the temple curtain was torn at the time of Jesus' death, it graphically and powerfully proclaimed the truth that the barrier between sinful persons and God had been removed by the sacrifice of Jesus.

Joseph of Arimathea and Nicodemus tenderly took down from the cross the body of Jesus and placed it in Joseph's tomb. The religious leaders sealed the tomb with a Roman seal. They set a guard about the tomb to secure his tomb from anyone who might try to steal His body. But all the forces of earth and hell could not keep Jesus in the tomb. By the mighty power of God He came forth in resurrection glory to guarantee resurrection power to all who believe in Him. Satan had bruised His heel on the cross, but in His resurrection He bruised the head of the serpent. He dealt the death blow to sin and Satan as He rose again. God's provision for salvation was complete.

People are confronted with the depth of their sin at the cross. They are offered the hope of forgiveness and new life through the power of the resurrection. Paul proclaimed, "I am not ashamed of the gospel, because it is the power of God for the salvation of everyone who believes: first for the Jew, then for the Gentile" (Rom. 1:16, NIV). On the divine side salvation has been accomplished. On the human side people must hear the good news and personally respond to Jesus Christ to be saved: " 'I tell you the truth, whoever hears my word and believes him who sent me has eternal life and will not be condemned; he has crossed over from death to life' " (John 5:24, NIV).

Although God's provision of salvation is universal, this does not imply that all will be saved. Some have concluded that since Christ died for all people, ultimately all will be saved. This is called the doctrine of universalism. Universalism is a deceitful heresy that offers false hope for humankind. Satan uses this heresy to lull multitudes into spiritual apathy. Universalism cuts the nerve of evangelistic urgency, causing churches and individual Christians to forsake the commission of Christ to share the gospel with every person.

Salvation is by faith in Christ only: "It is by grace you have been saved, through faith—and this not from yourselves, it is the gift of God—not by works, so that no one can boast" (Eph. 2:8-9, NIV). *Grace* has been defined as *the unmerited favor of God.* It is God's initiative as sovereign to give His Son to save all who will receive Him. It is God's act to reveal His salvation to every person who seeks Him with all his heart. Grace is God's saving love. It is a love we could never deserve, which God has given to us at great expense. Grace cost God the suffering and sacrifice of His Son.

This grace, God's gift, brings salvation: "The wages of sin is death, but the gift of God is eternal life in Christ Jesus our Lord" (Rom. 6:23, NIV). Jesus is the only way to life! Jesus said: " 'I am the way and the truth and the life. No one comes to the Father except through me' " (John 14:6, NIV). He is the true way to life. There is no other way! In his great sermon before the Sanhedrin Peter declared, " 'Salvation is found in no one else, for there is no other name under heaven given to men by which we must be saved' " (Acts 4:12, NIV). Apart from Christ every person is eternally lost.

Through Christ God revealed to a lost world His hatred for sin and His love for sinful humanity. By His grace God provided salvation for all humankind, and by His grace God has revealed His salvation. Salvation can come only through Jesus Christ. He is God's eternal provision for human lostness. The questions often arise: What about people who have never heard of Jesus? If God is loving and just, how can He condemn those who have never heard the good news? This is a legitimate question, but it is not easy to answer.

God has revealed Himself to all humankind in two ways, general revelation and special revelation.

What is meant by general revelation? One writer has explained it this way: "General revelation refers to the self-disclosure of God which all men can perceive by contemplating evidences of his existence and nature in the world of nature, history, and human life in general. The knowledge of God derived from this revelation is called the *natural knowledge of God.*"[1]

Through general revelation all people can know the reality of God's existence: "Because that which may be known of God is manifest in them; for God hath shewed it unto them. For the invisible things of him from the creation of the world are clearly seen, being understood by the things that are made, even his eternal power and Godhead; so that they are without excuse" (Rom. 1:19-20). All who refuse to respond to God's revelation in creation are without excuse.

In every person God has placed a moral and spiritual consciousness: "When the Gentiles, which have not the law, do by nature the things contained in the law, these, having not the law, are a law unto themselves: which shew the work of the law written in their hearts, their conscience also bearing witness, and their thoughts the mean while accusing or else excusing one another" (Rom. 2:14-15). The natural revelation of God through creation and through humans' inner consciousness is adequate to reveal their need for salvation and the reality of God's existence and presence. Yet no one can be saved through the light of natural revelation. Salvation is through Christ alone.

Special revelation, on the other hand, refers to God's revealing Himself in and through His mighty acts in the history of Israel and finally in Jesus Christ. Through His written Word, the Bible, God has revealed Himself. Through the witness of His church as it proclaims Jesus to the world, God reveals Himself and His salvation for humankind.

The special revelation of Christ to the heart and mind of a sinner is necessary for salvation. No one can be saved except by personal faith in Christ.

God responds to a seeking heart. He promised, " 'You will seek me and find me when you seek me with all your heart' " (Jer. 29:13, NIV). I believe that no matter where a person is, if he responds to the light God has given to seek the Lord with all his heart, God will provide additional light. He will not save the person apart from Christ, but He will send someone with the message of Christ to that person.

This happened in the case of Cornelius, a pagan Roman soldier, who sought the Lord with all his heart. God did not save him apart from Christ. Instead, God sent an angel to tell Cornelius to send for Simon Peter, who would tell him what to do. At the same time, God was dealing with Peter, who still believed that salvation was only for the Jews. God spoke to him through a vision of a sheet descending from heaven, filled with all kinds of animals that Peter considered unclean. The lesson was that Peter should not consider unclean what God had cleansed. At that moment the messengers from Cornelius arrived. Peter accompanied them to Cornelius and presented the gospel of Christ. Immediately, Cornelius believed and was saved (see Acts 10).

Often stories from the mission field have been told of missionaries who were impressed by God to go to specific places where the gospel had not been introduced. When they arrived, they found people who were seeking the Lord and were expecting someone to come to tell them the way. Their response in receiving Christ was immediate. This situation indicates that God works to create conviction and spiritual hunger, as well as to send His messenger with the truth of the gospel.

Ultimately, only God determines who is saved and who is lost. He alone is the judge of all people. The task of believers is to proclaim the gospel to all people. We can be certain that God is faithful. God is fair. If people continue in their lostness, it is because they have rejected the light that God has given them.

PERSONAL LEARNING ACTIVITY 8

Choose the statement that best describes what God has done to provide the way of salvation for you and others.

_____ 1. God has provided moral and ethical rules to help us live good lives.

_____ 2. God has provided forgiveness of sins and new life through the death of Jesus on the cross and His resurrection from the grave.

Not only has God by grace provided salvation in Christ, but He also by grace has clearly revealed the essential response by which persons can come to Christ and be saved. From the depths of His love for humankind God issued the call to personal salvation to "whosoever will." God's great desire is for everyone to be saved: "The Lord is not slow in keeping his promise, as some understand slowness. He is patient with you, not wanting anyone to perish, but everyone to come to repentance" (2 Pet. 3:9, NIV).

Two elements are present simultaneously in a conversion experience: repentance and faith. They are two sides of the same coin. Peter confronted his audience in Acts 3 with the admonition to repentance of their sins and to faith in Jesus as the Christ. When true repentance takes place in a life, it is accompanied by saving faith in Jesus Christ. Conversely, when a person believes in Christ with genuine, saving faith, repentance from sin is present. We will now examine repentance and the fact that they are required responses of human beings toward God. We will also look at the need for an open confession of faith and for believer's baptism.

Repentance toward God. W. T. Conner insightfully showed the relationship between repentance and faith in his book *Gospel Doctrines.*

Inseparably connected with repentance is faith in Christ as Savior and Lord. Repentance and faith go together. They are inseparable. They are not two acts or spiritual attitudes, but two aspects of one act or spiritual attitude. One does not repent and then believe in Christ, nor does he believe in Christ and then repent. Christ and sin are opposite poles of the moral universe, and one cannot turn from sin without turning to Christ as one phase of the same spiritual act any more than he can turn his face from the north without turning it toward the south.[2]

Yet for the sake of study, the meaning of and biblical instruction about both repentance and faith will be considered separately.

How important repentance is! Without repentance salvation is impossible (see Luke 13:3). "Easy believism" and shallow, superficial acceptance of Christ that make no difference in moral and ethical behavior and result in no commitment to the mission of Christ demand an adequate emphasis on repentance. The primary word in the New Testament for *repent* is the verb form *metanoew*. The verb is a combination of the preposition *meta (after)* and the verb *noew (understand, perceive, think over, consider)*. The noun *repentance (metanoia)* literally means *a change of mind.* It involves both attitude and action. An attitude toward sin of regret and godly sorrow leads to a change of action, a life-style of obedience to God that expresses real repentance.

The noted founder of Southern Baptist Theological Seminary, James P. Boyce, wrote that *metanoia*—

> traces the feeling of sorrow and the change of life back to an inward change of opinion and judgement as to the nature of sin and holiness, and of the relations of man and God. It is perhaps on this account that it is exclusively used for true repentance in the New Testament. This is not simply sorrow, or remorse, which may pass away, or lead in despair to other sins, or fill the soul with anxiety; but a heartfelt change in the inward soul towards God and holiness, which is lasting and effective, and which may be associated with peace and joy in believing.[3]

God's invitation to salvation is a call to radical change in a sinner's life. A person must experience the change of repudiating his own pride and accepting the forgiveness of God through Christ. He must experience the transformation of being made alive spiritually in Christ after being dead in sin. Such a life change has been termed conversion. Peter used the words *be converted* as he powerfully preached Jesus as the Christ to those who had crucified the Lord: " 'Repent ye therefore, and be converted, that your sins may be blotted out, when the times of refreshing shall come from the presence of the Lord' " (Acts 3:19).

A person's entire spiritual nature is involved in action when she repents. Repentance is an act of the intellect, emotion, and will. First, it is an act of the intellect. It is a change of thought. A person's attitude toward sin and toward God undergoes a change when she repents. Her thoughts about sin change from approval to disapproval. Her thoughts about God change from rebellion or indifference to acceptance and submission.

Second, repentance is an act of the emotions. A person's feelings change when he repents. He experiences godly sorrow for sin and a growing reverence and desire for God and His way.

Third, repentance is an act of the will. When a person repents, he volitionally turns from his sin to God. He finds new purpose in life. As an act of the will, he permanently repudiates sin and surrenders his life to God. He accepts God's attitude toward sin. Repentance manifests itself through the attitudes and actions of the person who has repented. Although salvation is not attained by human works, repentance shows itself through the works that result. However, it is never a mere outward display. Genuine repentance involves numerous outward evidences that in and of themselves are not repentance. It is not self-condemnation, self-depreciation, or the lack of self-esteem. A person may be filled with self-condemnation and have very low self-esteem and never repent. In fact, such an attitude may indicate that repentance has not been thorough and that cleansing from sin has not been experienced.

Repentance is not mere remorse or regret for sins committed. Judas acknowledged his sin and was filled with remorse; but obviously, he did not repent. True repentance does not turn the remorse for sin inward to punish oneself. It does not manifest itself in ascetic self-torture to alleviate a guilt complex. It turns to God for forgiveness.

Repentance is not simply human resolve to do better or the outward performance of religious rituals. Although repentance results in a new resolve and in joining a church and being baptized, it is more than these.

Genuine repentance manifests itself in numerous ways. The internal conflict of being at enmity with God is over. It results in an inner peace that knows the acceptance of God. It results in the joy of knowing that sin is forgiven. It creates the desire to right the wrongs committed. John the Baptist charged those who inquired about his preaching on repentance to go back and bring forth fruit worthy of repentance:

> "The man with two tunics should share with him who has none, and the one who has food should do the same."
>
> Tax collectors also came to be baptized. "Teacher," they asked, "what should we do?"
>
> "Don't collect any more than you are required to," he told them.
>
> Then some soldiers asked him, "And what should we do?"
>
> He replied, "Don't extort money and don't accuse people falsely—be content with your pay" (Luke 3:11-14, NIV).

Zacchaeus gave evidence of repentance in both attitude and action when he received Christ. Immediately, he promised Jesus that he would give half of his possessions to the poor and would restore to those he had cheated four times the amount (see Luke 19:8).

Repentance manifests itself in godly sorrow and confession of sin. When the presence of the holy God is realized, sin becomes apparent and appalling: " 'The tax collector stood at a distance. He would not even look up to heaven, but beat on his breast and said, "God, have mercy on me, a sinner" ' " (Luke 18:13, NIV). Jesus said that this man went home justified. Then He declared, " 'Everyone who exalts himself will be humbled, and he who humbles himself will be exalted' " (Luke 18:14, NIV). Today not enough is made of this manifestation of repentance.

The experience of repentance that results in conversion has been well illustrated by the life of one of my dear friends, Clifford. Today Clifford is a deacon and a leader in a great church. He is a faithful and a consistent witness for Christ. But when I met Clifford, he was at rock bottom in life. He had been a successful executive in a leading business. But through his ungodly life and addiction to alcohol he had disgraced his family and his company. After many attempts to reform him, the company had finally dismissed Clifford. Between periods of drinking he worked as a gasoline-station attendant. I met him on Saturday as he filled my car with gasoline. I spoke to him about Jesus and invited him to church. He indicated that he might come to church, and he did. Soon Clifford came to Christ, and God changed his life. Immediately, he became a different person. He left his old ways behind. He lived and testified for Christ. He was faithful to Christ and to his church. As Clifford shared his love for Christ, he would say, "Since I had my turnaround, my life has been different."

Years later, I asked Clifford what kept him from going back to the old life. His response revealed deep insight into the Christian life: "Since God gave me my turnaround, I keep on giving my testimony for Him." My friend's turnaround is what the Bible means by being converted. It is synonymous with being saved.

Repentance is effected by the message of the gospel of Christ. When the lost hear the gospel of Christ, the Holy Spirit does His work of conviction of sin, righteousness, and judgment (see John 16:8-11). As the lost one responds to the conviction of the Holy Spirit, he experiences contrition for sin, and conversion results as he turns to Christ. Genuine repentance is accompanied by saving faith in Jesus Christ.

P E R S O N A L   L E A R N I N G   A C T I V I T Y   9

Read the following statements carefully. Place a *T* beside any statement you believe to be true. Place an *F* beside any statement you believe to be false.

_____ 1. The primary meaning of *repentance* is *being sorry for sin.*
_____ 2. *Repentance* means *to turn from sin to God.*
_____ 3. It is necessary only to repent if you have done many things for which you feel guilty.
_____ 4. Every person must repent to be saved.

Faith in Jesus Christ. Both repentance and faith are gifts of God. Peter reported Cornelius's salvation to the churches with the following conclusion: " 'If God gave them the same gift as he gave us, who believed in the Lord Jesus Christ, who was I to think that I could oppose God?' When they heard this, they had no further objections and praised God, saying, 'So then, God has granted even the Gentiles repentance unto life' " (Acts 11:17-18, NIV).

Paul summarized the message he had proclaimed in Ephesus this way: " 'You know that I have not hesitated to preach anything that would be helpful to you but have taught you publicly and from house to house. I have declared to both Jews and Greeks that they must turn to God in repentance and have faith in our Lord Jesus' " (Acts 20:20, NIV).

What is saving faith? What is the meaning of faith? Faith is central in both the Old and New Testaments. "It is so rich in its contents, and so comprehensive, so inclusive of the relationships of man that it is easier to describe than it is to define it. All brief definitions of faith come short of the complete reality. Yet the meaning is simple and easy to grasp, in its essential content."[4]

The New Testament words that are commonly translated into English as *faith* and *believe* have the same Greek root. The noun *faith* is *pistis,* and the verb *believe* is *pisteou. Theological Dictionary of the New Testament* defines the word as *to believe, to obey, to trust, to hope,* and *faithfulness.*[5] It further presents faith as the acceptance of the content of the gospel and as a personal relationship with Christ. It has been rendered by various translations of the Bible as *believe, trust, rely on, cling to, adhere to, give assent to, commit to,* and *have confidence in.*

Like repentance, faith involves the response of a person's entire being to God as He has revealed Himself in Christ. The triune God Himself is the object of saving faith. Saving faith may be analyzed as three elements—an act of the intellect, of the emotions, and of the will—although it is impossible to separate one from the other. These elements are not necessarily in sequence, but they help us understand what takes place in a person's life when that person exercises faith in Jesus Christ.

The faith of a believer, first, has an intellectual element. It is believing the truth of the gospel. Paul outlined the basic content of the gospel in 1 Corinthians 15:3-8. It is the truth that Christ (the anointed one, the Messiah, the Son of God) "died for our sins according to the Scriptures, that he was buried, that he was raised on the third day according to the Scriptures, and that he appeared" (vv. 3-5, NIV) to Peter; to the twelve; to more than five hundred at one time; to James; and, last of all, to Paul himself. Faith is accepting God's provision for salvation as revealed historically in the Scriptures and the implications that the Bible gives for life. However, it is clear that mental assent alone to the gospel is not saving faith. Devils believe in this sense and tremble (see Jas. 2:10).

The faith of a believer, second, has an emotional element. The sinner, convicted of sin, recognizes his need for and God's provision of salvation. He responds by coming to Christ. Feeling as well as knowledge is involved in receiving Christ. Yet feeling by itself is inadequate for the experience of salvation. Jesus spoke of the emotional hearer as the stony-ground hearer whose faith would not continue (see Matt. 13:20-21).

The faith of a believer, third, has a volitional element. Faith is an act of the will. It involves the intellectual knowledge of the gospel and the emotional feeling of need for salvation, which result in trusting Christ and His provision. It is the deliberate, decisive act of casting oneself on the mercy of God and of depending totally on Him for salvation. It is the commitment of life and eternity to Jesus Christ.

The decision to receive Christ is so simple yet so difficult. It is so simple that a child can understand it. Yet it is so profoundly difficult that scholars may stumble. It is as simple as believing that God raised Jesus from the dead, receiving Him, and confessing Him as Lord (see Rom. 10:9). Herein lies the difficulty. It goes against the grain of sinful human pride to admit our absolute inability to do anything but receive Christ to be saved. It is difficult to yield to Him as Savior and Lord, who will then govern life. Since the garden of Eden, humans have wanted to do their own will rather than the will of God. Faith is yielding the control of one's life to Jesus Christ. It is committing one's life to Him as Lord.

Bill, a young engineer at NASA, had been regularly attending our services and was involved in our singles group. I witnessed to Bill several times. His response was always the same: "Pastor, I appreciate your concern, but I just cannot believe." One night I was in my office late. I had left the door to the hallway open. Bill passed by on his way to a singles activity. I called his name and asked him to come in for a moment. In the course of the conversation I asked if he had considered any further his decision to accept Christ. Bill gave the same excuse: "I have been trying, but I just cannot believe."

I turned to John 5:40 and asked him to read it: "Ye will not come to me, that ye might have life." Then I said: "Bill, do not say, 'I cannot believe.' You may say, 'I will not believe' but not 'I cannot believe.' You *can* believe if you *will.* God leaves that to you." Then I asked, "Will you believe that Jesus Christ is the Son of God?"

He waited, then answered slowly, "Yes, I will believe!"

I continued, "Will you believe that Christ died for your sins; rose again; and will save you if you call on Him, repenting of your sin and receiving Him?"

Again Bill said deliberately, "Yes, I will!"

The Holy Spirit was breaking down the barriers of pride in Bill's life through the convicting word of John 5:40. It was as if light was dawning in his heart and mind as he began to confess faith verbally.

My next question was the most difficult. I asked, "Will you bow with me and ask Him to forgive your sin and come into your life, and will you tell Him that you are committing your life to Him?"

Slipping from his chair to his knees, Bill replied, "Yes, I will!"

And he did! In that moment Bill came from death to life in Christ. With an expression of joy and gratitude he shook my hand, confessing his commitment to Jesus Christ. The next Sunday he confessed Christ as Lord publicly and was baptized. Bill, the young intellectual who could not believe, made the decision of his will to commit to Christ. Then he had no problem with intellectual belief. Bill had repented of his sin of rejecting Christ and had believed, commiting himself to the Savior.

Confession of Christ and baptism. Repentance and faith are manifested by obedience to Christ through confession of Christ as Lord and through baptism. John the Baptist called those who heard his preaching at the Jordan River to give outward expression to their repentance by being baptized (see Mark 1:4; Acts 13:24). Peter called those to whom he preached at Pentecost to " 'repent and be baptized, every one of you, in the name of Jesus Christ for the forgiveness of your sins' " (Acts 2:38, NIV). Baptism does not secure forgiveness. But the one who repents will desire to obey Christ by confessing His lordship and following Him in the outward act of baptism. Albert Barnes, in his commentary on Acts 2:38, has said about baptism: "It was equivalent to saying that they should *publicly* and *professedly* embrace Jesus Christ as their Saviour. The gospel requires such a profession, and no one is at liberty to withhold it. . . . If men are unwilling to profess religion they have none."[6] Confession of Christ and baptism are vital parts of the response God expects from those who come to Him for salvation.

Confessing Jesus as Lord. A biblical passage that is often quoted in regard to conversion is Romans 10:9-10: "If you confess with your mouth, 'Jesus is Lord,' and believe in your heart that God raised him from the dead, you will be saved. For it is with your heart that you believe and are justified, and it is with your mouth that you confess and are saved" (NIV). People often emphasize the part of the passage that speaks of believing with the heart, while ignoring the part that speaks of confessing with the mouth. When people do this, they fail to take God's Word seriously. As certainly as people are told in this passage to believe, they are instructed to confess. The confession that is required is "Jesus is Lord."

What does this mean in a practical sense? How does one confess that Jesus is Lord? Because confession of Christ is commanded in God's Word, these are important questions. Invitations to accept Christ are frequently given in Southern Baptist and other evangelical churches. Persons are invited to step forward, walk down the aisle, and thereby signal their intentions to follow Christ as Savior and Lord. Many people have found this practice of public invitation helpful. Certainly, it is right to call people to a decision about the gospel. But confessing Christ as Lord means more than walking down an aisle at invitation time.

The way of salvation that God has provided is the gift of His grace. No person can earn or deserve this gift. It is freely given by God and does not depend on works. Yet to accept that gift involves committing one's life to Jesus. Pastors, teachers, evangelists, and others who seek to lead people to Christ should impress on those to whom they witness that becoming a Christian involves confessing that Jesus is Lord and that accepting Him means turning over their lives to Him.

A new believer will not be able to understand everything that confessing Jesus as Lord means. Confessing Jesus as Lord and understanding what His lordship means are parts of an ongoing process. True conversion, however, must begin from the point of commitment to Jesus, and this involves confessing His lordship.

When persons respond to a public invitation or make a decision as a result of a personal witness, they should be led to confess openly that Jesus is Lord. It should be made clear to such persons that saying, "Jesus is Lord" involves more than words. This confession is not an empty formality. Rather, confessing the lordship of Christ expresses the essential meaning of the salvation experience. Coming to God for salvation involves repentance, turning from a self-centered, Christ-rejecting way of life. Coming to God for salvation also involves faith, accepting God's provision for salvation in Christ, and committing one's life to Him.

The call to salvation is never to a tentative or partial commitment. Conversion always involves bringing all we understand of ourselves in surrender to what we understand of Jesus. The ongoing process of confessing Jesus as Lord is discipleship, following Him. A person must begin the Christian life with an attitude of confessing Him as Lord, even though it takes a lifetime of following Him to understand the implications of that confession.

Believer's baptism. Baptism is a meaningful, beautiful way to confess publicly that Jesus is Lord. Baptists have sometimes reacted so strongly to the heresy of baptismal regeneration that they have ignored the importance of baptism. The waters of baptism have no saving power. Only Christ can save. But baptism is an important symbol and confession of everything that salvation is. Paul wrote in Romans 6:3-4: "Don't you know that all of us who were baptized into Christ Jesus were baptized into his death? We were therefore buried with him through baptism into death in order that, just as Christ was raised from the dead through the glory of the Father, we too may live a new life" (NIV).

When one is baptized by immersion, that person publicly identifies with the death, burial, and resurrection of Christ and publicly confesses that in the power of the resurrection he intends to live a new life.

The only proper candidate for baptism is a believer. The only mode of baptism that preserves its meaning is immersion. The meaning of baptism is that the person being baptized is dying to sin and rising to a new life in Christ.

Baptists refer to baptism as an ordinance because baptism is commanded by Christ (see Matt. 28:19). It is unthinkable that any believer who is instructed in what baptism means would not be eager to confess Christ in this meaningful way.

P E R S O N A L   L E A R N I N G   A C T I V I T Y   10

What do you understand *baptism* to mean? Write your answer below. Use another sheet of paper if necessary.

_____

_____

_____

_____

_____

_____

_____

_____

Salvation: A Perspective on Children

There is something especially wonderful about a child's accepting Jesus because a child has a lifetime to follow and serve Jesus. Many Christian leaders testify that they came to the Savior as children, often as very young children. It is common in Baptist churches to see young children decide to trust Jesus and follow Him in baptism.

Jesus loved children, and they responded to Him with love. We are familiar with the beautiful story in Mark 10:13-16. The disciples mistakenly attempted to prevent children from being brought to Jesus. Jesus became indignant and rebuked His disciples: " 'Let the little children come to me, and do not hinder them, for the kingdom of God belongs to such as these' " (v. 14, NIV). The childlike trust and willingness to love that are so precious in children are, in fact, attitudes anyone who comes to Jesus must have. Children should never be discouraged or hindered from coming to Jesus.

Yet children must be led gently and instructed thoroughly in making the most important decision of their lives. Children must never be pressured, manipulated, or hurried to make professions of faith.

We often speak of the age of accountability. This expression refers to the age at which a person becomes responsible to God in the matter of salvation. Robert Sloan expresses the view that the age of accountability means more than the age when a child knows the difference between right and wrong. He suggests that we should think of the age of gospel accountability. He defines this age as "that point in human development when the child is both morally and intellectually capable of understanding the *gospel* (the story of Christ's death for our sins and His resurrection) and either receive that message in faith or reject it."[7]

The age of gospel accountability does not correspond directly to a chronological age. A child's understanding, stage of development, and early exposure to the gospel are more important than age.

Parents, teachers, pastors, and other Christians who relate to children should think in terms of nurturing children rather than hurrying them to make a decision they do not understand and are not ready to make. A biblical model is found in 2 Timothy 3:14-15. Paul urged Timothy to continue in what he had learned of the Christian faith "because you know those from whom you learned it, and how from infancy you have known the holy Scriptures, which are able to make you wise for salvation through faith in Christ Jesus." We are not told at what age Timothy was saved; but we know that the nurture he received in childhood led him to that all-important moment when he accepted Christ as his own Lord and Savior.

Not every child is blessed with a spiritually nurturing home like that of Timothy. Sunday School teachers, pastors, and other Christians have a tremendous responsibility to children, especially those who do not grow up in Christian homes. Children must be loved, taught, and gently led to Jesus as they come to the time in their lives when they understand the gospel. The Holy Spirit will work in the lives of children to bring them to that moment of decision. Older Christians must not hurry children to make a decision.

Another important point to remember about the conversion of children is that children will make a decision for Christ on a child's level. Since they have not experienced years of sinful living, they should not be expected to react in the same way as an adult, who has to deal with years of rebellion and sin. A child may express his decision mainly in terms of trusting Jesus, loving Jesus, and letting Jesus be Savior and friend. This does not make the child's decision less real. Children who make professions of faith should be carefully counseled to help them understand the decision that has been made. Of course, this counseling will need to use terminology and concepts the child can understand. Following the profession of faith, the child should be taught, encouraged, and nurtured in the Christian life.

PERSONAL LEARNING ACTIVITY 11

Choose the statement that you feel describes a child's age of accountability.

_____ 1. A child is accountable at the age of 12.

_____ 2. A child is accountable when the child knows the difference between right and wrong.

_____ 3. A child is accountable when the child is morally and intellectually able to understand the gospel.

Conclusion
God has provided salvation for all who call on Him in repentance and faith. In summary, saving faith involves the following.
- Hearing the Word (see Rom. 10:17)
- Conviction of need (see John 16:8-11)
- Repenting of sin (see Rom. 2:4)
- Believing in Christ and receiving Him (see John 1:12)
- Confessing Christ as Lord (see Rom. 10:9)
- Baptism and commitment to a church (see Acts 2:38-41)

Although baptism and church commitment are not essential to salvation, they are obedient, outward expressions of a genuine salvation experience. Salvation results in following Jesus Christ as a disciple (see Matt. 16:24).

Salvation is not do!

Salvation is not don't!

Salvation is done!

The work of our salvation is the finished work of Christ on the cross! Whosoever will, let him come.

DOCTRINE IN LIFE

This week do one of the following activities.

1. Observe a baptismal service in your church and make notes on how the meaning of baptism is explained at the service.
2. Interview your pastor, a staff minister, or a deacon. Ask how candidates for baptism are counseled in your church. How is baptism explained to these candidates?

---

[1]Shirley C. Guthrie, Jr., *Christian Doctrine* (Richmond: Covenant Life Curriculum Press, 1968), 56.

[2]W. T. Conner, *Gospel Doctrines* (Nashville: Sunday School Board of the Southern Baptist Convention, 1925), 89.

[3]James P. Boyce, *Abstract of Systematic Theology* (n.p.: Christian Gospel Foundation, 1887), 383.

[4]E. Y. Mullins, *The Christian Religion in Its Doctrinal Expression* (Philadelphia: Judson Press, 1917), 371.

[5]Gerhard Friedrich, ed., *Theological Dictionary of the New Testament* (Grand Rapids: William B. Eerdmans Publishing Company, 1968), 205-8.

[6]Albert Barnes, *Notes on the New Testament: Acts* (Grand Rapids: Baker Book House, 1981), 53.

[7]Robert Sloan, "Baptists and Children," *Exploring 1 for Leaders*, July, August, September 1986, 4.

The New Birth

QUESTIONS TO GUIDE YOUR STUDY
1. *What does* born again *mean?*
2. *Why is the new birth an essential experience?*
3. *How does the new birth relate to daily living?*

"Born again? What do you mean?" This was the bewildered response of some reporters several years ago when presidential candidate Jimmy Carter asserted during press interviews that he had been born again. It was reported that a religion editor of a leading metropolitan newspaper phoned a noted church historian and talked with him for an hour, trying to gain insight into this concept of being born again.

In the wake of the Jimmy Carter interviews, many claimed to be born again. A poll taken at that time indicated that every third American 18 years of age and older said that he or she had been born again.

With the popularization of the term, experiences of many kinds began to be reported as born-again experiences. What does it mean to say that one has been born again? This question is important because the new birth is at the heart of the experience of salvation. We must look to the teaching of Scripture to discover the truth about the new birth.

The New Birth: The New Testament Witness

Jesus introduced the term *born again* to Nicodemus, an intellectual of that day. Nicodemus was as mystified as any modern person could be when Jesus said to him, " 'I tell you the truth, no one can see the kingdom of God unless he is born again' " (John 3:3, NIV). Nicodemus's immediate and spontaneous response indicated his certainty that being born a second time is utterly impossible: " 'How can a man be born when he is old? . . . Surely he cannot enter a second time into his mother's womb to be born!' " (John 3:4, NIV). Nicodemus used the term *dunatai (is possible)*, preceded by the negative particle *me (not)*, to indicate that he expected a negative answer. *Dunatai* comes from the same root as the noun *dunamis (power)*, from which we get our word *dynamite.* Literally, Nicodemus was asking: "No one can possibly enter into his mother's womb and be born a second time, can he? It is impossible, isn't it? No one has that kind of power, does he?" Unconsciously and unintentionally, the puzzled Nicodemus stated a central truth. Human beings cannot accomplish a new birth. The new birth is a miraculous work of God.

Jesus' term *born again* reflects both the miracle and the mystery of the experience. His term *born* is a form of the verb *gennao*, which means *to beget, to generate*, or *to bring into being. Again* is the word *anothen.* It has the possibility of a dual meaning *(again* or *anew* and *from above).* It could refer to a second physical birth or to the complete, radical change of a supernatural birth from above.

Nicodemus understood Jesus to be referring to a second physical birth. Herschel H. Hobbs says that Jesus was using—

"shock treatment" . . . to dislodge from Nicodemus's thinking the idea that he was already in the kingdom of God by virtue of his *first* natural birth. . . . A Jew believed that he did not need to gain entrance into the kingdom of God. He was automatically in it by his natural birth. Thereafter, his good works were merely to make him well pleasing to God, the result being greater rewards in the kingdom.

Now Nicodemus is faced with a birth, *anothen.* A second physical birth, you say? Surely you cannot mean that. How? The shock method had worked. Bewildered, the Pharisee asks for further light.[1]

Paul used a synonym for *born again* in Titus 3:5, the word *palingenesia*, translated *regeneration.* Literally, it means *a new genesis* or *birth from above.* It has the idea of coming back from death to life.

A key word in relating the new-birth experience is the word *change.* The new birth brings a radical change. Repentance and faith are the human responses in conversion to God's provision of salvation through Christ. The regenerating new birth is God's miraculous work through the Holy Spirit in the life of the one who turns to Him.

The word picture of a new birth is one of the most graphic and dramatic in all literature. It holds a central place in the New Testament. John introduced it in the first chapter of his Gospel (see John

1:12-13). Every verse in the account of Nicodemus's encounter with Jesus is pregnant with truth about it. Volumes could be and have been written, based on these concise, direct words of Jesus. The new birth is referred to in 1 John 2:29; 3:9; 4:7; 5:1,4,18. Peter wrote about the new birth in 1 Peter 1:3,23. Paul wrote about the experience of regeneration in Titus 3:5.

The same truth is expressed through other terms in many places in the New Testament. It is expressed as "a new creation" (2 Cor. 5:17, NIV), the crucified, risen life (see Gal. 2:20), being transformed (see Rom. 12:2), "the new self" (Eph. 4:24, NIV), being made alive (see Eph. 2:5), and being dead to sin and alive to God (see Rom. 6:1-6). The entire teaching in the New Testament on the new life in Christ is based on the experience of the new birth.

PERSONAL LEARNING ACTIVITY 12

How does Jesus' insistence to Nicodemus that a person be born again contrast with the idea that an individual is part of God's kingdom by natural birth? Write your answer on the lines provided or on a separate sheet of paper.

_____

_____

_____

_____

_____

_____

The New Birth: The Essential Experience

Truths given in the account of Nicodemus's interview with Jesus in John 3 and other passages give insight into the meaning of the new birth. The Scriptures clearly teach that the new birth is essential to a right relationship with God.

Futile substitutes. Lost persons use many and various methods to try to justify themselves. Nicodemus is a classic example. He was very religious. He was a Pharisee, a leader, and a teacher of religion. He was so entrenched in his religion that he knew he was right. But Jesus chided him with the fact that although he was a teacher in Israel, he had missed the very basis of spiritual life. Today many people become involved in a religion and, by religious affiliation and participation, attempt to justify themselves before God.

Morality is another means people use to justify themselves before God. It is right and commendable to live an upright, honest, moral life. Nicodemus, without doubt, was one of the finest moral men of his time; but morality alone does not justify a person before God.

Some cling to an experience in life to claim justification before God. One woman said, "God saved me from a car wreck; therefore, I know that I am saved." Although it is true that God works in many ways in our lives, these experiences do not necessarily mean that a person is saved.

Still others depend on family relationships or nationality for justification. This was part of Nicodemus's problem. He believed that since he was an Israelite, born to a good Jewish family, he was right with God. Today some people think that because their parents were Christians, their father was a deacon or a preacher, and they were brought up in church, they are Christians also. But unless one is born again personally, he is not saved.

Human hindrances. Humankind's ideas of God and salvation are distorted. Human beings misunderstand the nature of God and supernatural, divine power. Nicodemus asked, " 'How can this be?' " (John 3:9, NIV). To the natural mind the new birth is an impossibility because of its mystery. How foolish! People accept other mysteries, although they cannot explain them. Jesus used the illustration of the blowing wind (see John 3:8). No one knows where it comes from or where it goes. Yet we know that it is blowing. The evidences are there. We feel it. We see the evidences of it in rustling leaves, blowing sands, and tossing waves. Just so is the spiritual birth. It is humanly unexplainable, yet the evidence is there when it happens. Inner change occurs. It is experienced and verified by a changed life.

In everyday life we experience the unexplainable. In my room are sounds and pictures that I cannot hear with my natural ear or see with my natural eye. But I know that they are there. I have a television set in my room. When I turn on the power, it receives the sound and pictures so I can hear and see them. They are there, whether or not I realize it. My ignorance of them does not negate their reality. Similarly, the spiritual ignorance of the natural person keeps him from experiencing the things of God.

Not only are lost people spiritually dead, but also their minds cannot comprehend spiritual truth: "The man without the Spirit does not accept the things that come from God, for they are foolishness to him, and he cannot understand them, because they are spiritually discerned. The spiritual man makes judgments about all things, but he himself is not subject to any man's judgment: 'For who has known the mind of the Lord that he may instruct him?' But we have the mind of Christ" (1 Cor. 2:14-16, NIV). A person who is born again receives the things of God and communes with God because Christ lives in him. Such a person's mind is spiritually in tune with God. But the natural mind is closed to God's Spirit. It is like a radio receiver that is set on a different frequency. The human mind is not tuned in to God. Therefore, it does not receive the things of God.

Human pride is another hindrance that keeps persons from experiencing the new birth. People desire to be the gods of their own lives. Therefore, they attempt to justify themselves before God. The first man born on earth, Cain, determined to come to God his own way rather than God's way (see Gen. 4:3-7). His attitude was "What do I care what God requires? I will offer God what I please. I will come to God my own way." People continue to follow the pattern of Cain when they say: "There are many ways to reach God. I will come to God the way I choose."

Paul pointed out that this same pride kept the Jews of his day from Christ: "Since they did not know the righteousness that comes from God and sought to establish their own, they did not submit to God's righteousness. Christ is the end of the law so that there may be righteousness for everyone who believes" (Rom. 10:3-4, NIV). People still seek to establish their own righteousness and justify themselves before God.

Divine transaction. The new birth may be explained as a transaction, one that can be accomplished only by God Himself in a person's life. It is demanded both by the nature of God and by the nature of human beings. God is holy. He is above sin. Human beings in their sinful state cannot approach God until change has been wrought. At the judgment of the great white throne in Revelation 20:11 we are told that the "earth and sky fled from his presence, and there was no place for them" (NIV). We are told too that " 'God is spirit, and his worshipers must worship in spirit and in truth' " (John 4:24). Lost human beings are spiritually dead. They are incapable of worshiping God in spirit and truth. The Scripture asks: "What do righteousness and wickedness have in common? Or what fellowship can light have with darkness?" (2 Cor. 6:14). Lost human beings are in darkness, incapable of having fellowship with the God of light. The nature of God demands that persons change spiritually to come together with God in intimate communion.

Not only does the nature of God demand the new birth, but human nature also makes it imperative. In their natural state human beings are spiritually dead: "As for you, you were dead in your transgressions and sins" (Eph. 2:1, NIV). It is impossible for one who is dead to communicate with or participate in the life of a living God. Human beings cannot enliven themselves. Christ is our life source. Until He enters the life of the sinner to forgive sin and through the Holy Spirit to transact the new birth, all people remain spiritually dead, separated from God.

The new birth is a divine transaction. A person must be born from above. The lost condition of humankind necessitates God's divine activity in the human heart to prepare persons to receive the truth. As slaves in sin (see John 8:34), persons need deliverance from the powers of darkness (see Col. 1:13), and only the miracle of the new birth can accomplish this deliverance.

The New Birth: The Work of the Spirit

God uses three elements to draw sinners to Himself: the work of the Spirit, the Word of God, and the witness of the believer. The influence of the Spirit of God initiates the birth from above: " 'No one can come to me unless the Father who sent me draws him, and I will raise him up at the last day. It is written in the Prophets: "They will all be taught by God. Everyone who listens to the Father and learns from him comes to me" ' " (John 6:44-45, NIV). The Holy Spirit acts in the heart and mind of the sinner to draw him to Christ. He works to create a spiritual hunger and thirst for true righteousness. Nicodemus manifested such a desire when he came to Jesus by night.

The Holy Spirit acts to accomplish His work through the Word of God. He inspired the Word and sends it forth to accomplish His holy purpose (see Isa. 55:11; John 14:26; 2 Tim. 3:16). He sends forth His witnesses equipped with His offensive weapon, the sword of the Spirit (see Eph. 6:17), for spiritual warfare with the enemy to deliver human souls. Like a two-edged sword, the Word has mighty power to penetrate deep into the hearts and souls of persons: "The word of God is living and active. Sharper than any double-edged sword, it penetrates even to dividing soul and spirit, joints and marrow; it judges the thoughts and attributes of the heart" (Heb. 4:12, NIV).

Through the Word of God the Holy Spirit does a threefold work of convicting the lost of their guilt and need for Christ. First, He convicts of the sin of not believing in Christ. Second, He convicts of righteousness, revealing the righteousness of Christ to the heart. Third, He convicts of judgment because the prince of this world has already been judged and stands condemned. The Holy Spirit guides the mind of the lost to realize their lostness and condemnation (see John 16:8-11).

Spiritual enlightenment of the mind with the truth of the gospel is accomplished by the Holy Spirit. Until the mind that has been darkened by the god of this world has been enlightened by the Spirit, a person cannot receive Christ. But when the Holy Spirit has done His work of enlightenment, a person is capable of responding to Christ. I had witnessed to a young man several times. His response was courteous but somewhat indifferent. Later, I shared the gospel with him again. Everything was different. It was as if the light had been switched on in his heart and mind. The Holy Spirit had done His work of enlightening. The man received Christ and continued to follow Him.

The work of the Holy Spirit is central in effecting the new birth. The mediation of salvation is a Holy Spirit work. A fivefold work of the Holy Spirit takes place in a life that is born again. The Spirit is the key to effectiveness and victory in the Christian life.

Imparts life to believers. First, the believer is born of the Spirit. Christ enters the heart through the person of the Spirit. The believer does not receive Christ at one time and at a later time receive the Holy Spirit: "You, however, are controlled not by the sinful nature but by the Spirit, if the Spirit of God lives in you. And if anyone does not have the Spirit of Christ, he does not belong to Christ" (Rom. 8:9, NIV). The Spirit does the transforming miracle of birthing a person into the kingdom of God. Through His divine power He imparts the spiritual nature of God into the heart of the believer.

The new birth is a one-time, irreversible act of the Spirit. When one is born again, she enters a permanent relationship as a child of the Father.

Indwells believers. Second, when one is born again, the Spirit indwells her life: "Do you not know that your body is a temple of the Holy Spirit, who is in you, whom you have received from God? You are not your own; you were bought with a price. Therefore honor God with your body" (1 Cor. 6:19-20, NIV). The indwelling Spirit enables the believer to commune with the Father in prayer: "The Spirit helps us in our weakness. We do not know what we ought to pray for, but the Spirit himself intercedes for us with groans that words cannot express" (Rom. 8:26, NIV). Prayer becomes meaningful and powerful, and the believer is guided and energized. God is honored through His people's prayers.

The indwelling Spirit brings comfort to the heart of the child of God. Jesus promised His disciples that He would not leave them comfortless like orphans. He promised to come in the person of the Comforter, who would live in them (see John 14:16-18). The word *Comforter* may be translated *Strengthener.* The strengthening presence of the Spirit is true comfort. The work of comforting is not a work of removing all difficulties so that one lives in passive ease. It is the inner strengthening of the Spirit to enable the believer to face hardships with victory.

The indwelling Spirit enables and empowers the witness of the believer (see Acts 1:8). He guides the witness to the lost person who needs the gospel. He gives the message of Christ with boldness through the witnessing believer.

Baptizes believers. Third, when one is born again, he is baptized by the Spirit: "We were all baptized by one Spirit into one body—whether Jews or Greeks, slave or free—and we were all given the one Spirit to drink" (1 Cor. 12:13, NIV). The baptism of the Spirit is not evidenced by any particular gift. He is Himself the salvation gift (see Acts 2:38). It is not the exclusive gift of a select few superspiritual people. In the Corinthian letters Paul wrote to all types of believers. They possessed various gifts and abilities. Some were immature. Some were carnal and quarrelsome. Some were engaged in questionable activities. Yet Paul said that all were baptized by the Spirit.

Through the baptism of the Spirit the believer is incorporated into the body of Christ. He is baptized into union with Christ and into unity with all believers in the body. Thus, he becomes one with Christ and with those who are His.

Seals believers. Fourth, when one is born again, he is sealed by the Holy Spirit: "You also were included in Christ when you heard the word of truth, the gospel of your salvation. Having believed, you were marked in him with a seal, the promised Holy Spirit, who is a deposit guaranteeing our inheritance until the redemption of those who are God's own possession—to the praise of his glory" (Eph. 1:13-14, NIV). The Spirit is the seal, stamp, or mark of God in the believer's life. The seal of the Spirit denotes three tremendous realities, which can be seen in the way the word was used in New Testament times.

A king used his signet ring to make an impression in wax on a document to designate it as official. The Holy Spirit is God's seal, designating that the believer has become a part of His family. We have received the Spirit of adoption (see Rom. 8:23). The adoption is official, legally accepted in the court of eternity.

The word for *seal* was used to describe the act of an owner of an animal when he branded or placed his mark on the animal. Branding animals still designates ownership. The Holy Spirit is God's mark in the life of the believer to designate that this one belongs to God.

The word *seal* was used as a guarantee. The Holy Spirit in the life of the believer is God's seal or guarantee that God will complete our redemption. When we place a postage stamp on a letter, the postal service guarantees that the letter will get to the destination to which it was addressed. God places His stamp in our lives to guarantee that He will get us to the point and place that He promised. He will complete what He has begun.

Fills believers. Fifth, when a believer is born again, he is filled with the Holy Spirit. When sin is confessed and Christ is received, the life is cleansed, and the Spirit comes in to take control. The command of Ephesians 5:18 is "Be filled with the Spirit." The filling of the Spirit is available to believers on a continuing basis. This filling equips the Christian for powerful witness and ministry.

The first four transactions of the Spirit are once for all and nonrecurring: one spiritual birth, one indwelling, one baptism, and one sealing of the Spirit. But there are many fillings. One is filled with the Spirit at conversion, but the fullness may not be maintained. Being filled with the Spirit may best be understood as being controlled or directed by the Spirit. When a child of God is disobedient and sin controls his life, he is no longer filled with the Spirit.

The present tense of the word that is translated *be filled* in Ephesians 5:18 denotes continuous action. The translation may literally and accurately be "Keep on being filled with the Spirit." Being filled with the Spirit is a daily, moment-by-moment walk of obedience with the Father.

When sin has come into the life of a Christian and he is no longer filled with the Spirit, the fullness can be restored. A Christian does not have to continue in disobedience and spiritual defeat. He may confess his sin and be forgiven and cleansed (see 1 John 1:9). Then he may yield once again to the control of the Spirit and continue in obedience to Him. An outstanding Christian layman has the motto "Confess and be filled." Here is the secret to victorious living. It is the Holy Spirit who initiates and enables the Christian life.

PERSONAL LEARNING ACTIVITY 13

Review the section "Baptizes believers." Place a *T* beside each statement that you believe is true. Place an *F* beside each statement that you believe is false.

____ The baptism of the Holy Spirit is an experience that only certain Christians have.

____ Every Christian is baptized by the Spirit.

____ The baptism of the Holy Spirit is always evidenced by the expression of an outstanding spiritual gift.

____ Through the baptism of the Holy Spirit, believers are incorporated into the body of Christ.

The New Birth: Characteristics

The new birth is a miracle that only God can bring to pass. It is so all-encompassing and deep in meaning that our categories of thought could never describe or contain it. However, several terms help describe the new birth.

Transition. The miracle of the new birth demands a divine transition. Only God can do what is required within a person to effect the miraculous work of regeneration. It is indeed a birth from above.

The new birth may be explained as a transition from death to life. It is a transition involving the greatest power in the universe, the power to bring the dead to life. In the new birth God makes alive the one who was dead in trespasses and sins. Humans have no power to give spiritual life. Jesus Christ is the life-giver. Through the Holy Spirit He enlivens the person who comes to Him in repentance and faith: "To all who received him, to those who believed in his name, he gave the right to become children of God" (John 1:12, NIV). The seed of God's Word has been planted into the heart, and the Holy Spirit brings life to one who was dead: "You have been born again, not of perishable seed, but of imperishable, through the living and enduring word of God" (1 Pet. 1:23, NIV).

Nicodemus stumbled at Jesus' mention of this miracle. He could not comprehend a birth from above. He interpreted Jesus' words as referring to a second physical birth (see John 3:4). Jesus instructed him in the nature of the spiritual birth: " 'I tell you the truth, no one can enter the kingdom of God unless he is born of water and the Spirit. Flesh gives birth to flesh, but the Spirit gives birth to spirit' " (John 3:5-6, NIV). Jesus conveyed the truth that through the natural human or "flesh birth" no person can enter the kingdom of God. Thus, He got to the heart of Nicodemus's problem. His physical birth as a Jew and his human relationships were not adequate to make him a child of God. A person is born physically to become a member of the human family, but he must be born spiritually to become a child of God.

The use of the word *water* in John 3:5 has resulted in three major interpretations. Those who teach a doctrine of baptismal regeneration use this verse to prove that a person must be baptized to be saved. Such an interpretation contradicts the scriptural doctrine of salvation by grace through faith. It violates the immediate context of John 3 and the teaching of the entire New Testament. We should never minimize the importance of baptism as an outward profession of faith in the death, burial, and resurrection of Christ and as a declaration of the believer's death to sin and resurrection to a new life in Christ. But baptism does not save.

Others interpret the reference to water in John 3:5 in terms of the experience of cleansing and renewing by the Word of God and by the Holy Spirit. Whether or not the term *water* is used that way here, it is true that people are cleansed and spiritually renewed through the Word of God and the work of the Holy Spirit.

Another interpretation is that the word *water* refers to the physical birth. Jesus intensified His teaching by using parallelism, or repetition of the truth in another form, when He said, " 'Flesh gives birth to flesh' " (John 3:6, NIV).

Herschel H. Hobbs concludes that "however one may read 'water and Spirit' in verse 5, it is clear that in verse 6 Jesus contrasts the natural and spiritual births."[2]

In John 5:24 Jesus reiterated the transition from death to life when one is born again: " 'I tell you the truth, whoever hears my word and believes him who sent me has eternal life and will not be condemned; he has crossed over from death to life' " (NIV). What a glorious reality! The person who is born again has eternal spiritual life and will never be condemned.

Paul interpreted the believer's transition from death to life in Romans 6, in which believers are identified with Christ in His death. Baptism is emblematic of planting a life in Christ. The old life, crucified with Christ, is dead. Sin has no dominion over a dead person. A person who has died to self is not under the law but under grace. By grace God has resurrected her with Christ to a new life. The newborn believer has been delivered from the slavery of sin and Satan.

Transformation. The new birth may be explained as a transformation. It is an internal spiritual transformation, resulting in a new heart. The Old Testament prophets set forth the need and promise of a new heart for the people of God. A person has no capacity to transform his own life and create within himself a new heart:

> Can the Ethiopian change his skin
> or the leopard its spots?
> Neither can you do good
> who are accustomed to doing evil (Jer. 13:23, NIV).

Whether it is a Nicodemus with an outstanding moral life or a Samaritan woman who has had five husbands and is living with a man to whom she is not married, every person needs a change of heart. No one can transform his or her heart. Transformation is a divine change.

God promised a new heart in Ezekiel 36:26: " ' "I will give you a new heart and put a new spirit in you; I will remove from you your heart of stone and give you a heart of flesh" ' " (NIV; also see Ezek. 11:19). The promise is fulfilled in the new birth. By grace through faith God creates a new person in Christ for the purpose of doing good works (see Eph. 2:8-10): "If anyone is in Christ, he is a new creation; the old is gone, the new has come!" (2 Cor. 5:17, NIV). The *King James Version* reads, "All things are become new." There is a new purpose to do God's will and to please Him. There is a new desire for a pure heart and a godly life. There is a new direction, living under the leadership of the Holy Spirit. There is a new mission to be an ambassador for Christ, witnessing to others and reaching the world for Christ. Nothing apart from a new creation can make all things new.

The new creation is "in Christ." In Ephesians 1 Paul enumerated the "spiritual blessings" the believer has "inherited" in Christ. In Christ the believer is "holy and blameless" (v. 4, NIV). He is "adopted as his son" (v. 5, NIV). He has "redemption through his blood, the forgiveness of sins" (v. 7, NIV). He has "knowledge" of the mystery of his will (v. 8, NIV). He has received the "seal" of the Holy Spirit (v. 13, NIV). He has an "inheritance" with the Father (v. 14, NIV). The believer has the power "to grasp how wide and long and high and deep is the love of Christ, and to know this love that surpasses knowledge"

(Eph. 3:18-19, NIV).

Because the new has come in Christ through the transformation of the new birth, the old is left behind. The believer now has the power in Christ to overcome the world by refusing to be conformed to the world but by continuing to be transformed by the renewing of the mind (see Rom. 12:2). Victory in daily living is possible through the transforming power of Christ in the believer.

Human resolution or reformation could never accomplish in a sinner's heart the transformation that the Holy Spirit generates in the new birth. Religion, reformation, and rule keeping can cleanse only the outward person. Nicodemus was blind and blind to the fact that he was blind. He was dead and unaware of the fact that he was dead. He was lost and lost to the fact that he was lost. The transforming work of the Holy Spirit is essential for the new birth.

Justification. The new birth may be explained as a change of position. Positionally, the lost person is separated from God, under sin and condemned. When he turns to Christ and is born again, he has a new position before God. He is justified by God Himself: "Since we have been justified through faith, we have peace with God through our Lord Jesus Christ" (Rom. 5:1, NIV). Justification is the act of God in declaring the sinner as righteous. Sin is forgiven, guilt is remitted, and the sinner is given right standing before God.

Justification is a legal term. The word *justification* is the New Testament word *dikaiosis.* The word carries the sense *to vindicate* or *to declare to be righteous.* A form of this word is used in Romans 4, in which Paul said that Abraham was not justified by works; but Abraham believed God, and it was credited to him for righteousness (see Rom. 4:3). The human attitude is that to be justified, one must do good works worthy of justification. But God does not act as humans act. Romans 4:5 declares, "To the man who does not work but trusts God who justifies the wicked, his faith is credited as righteousness" (NIV).

Sinful humans ought to be condemned to eternal hell. By their own merit they should be lost forever. But God, who is rich in mercy, has provided salvation in Christ. When the sinner believes in Christ, he is born again and declared by God as righteous. A person is like a defendant in court whose verdict is guilty. But the judge declares him not guilty. Likewise, God sees the faith of the believer and renders the verdict not guilty. Christ bore the guilt of sinful humanity on the cross. He took the punishment for human sin on Himself. A born-again person is in Christ. When God looks on a sinful person who has come by faith to Christ, He does not see a person in his sin. He sees the righteousness of Christ and the blood of His Son covering the person's sin. God is "just, and the justifier of him which believeth in Jesus" (Rom. 3:26).

Justification is the basis for a peace relationship with God and for beginning the new life. Paul made a captivating statement about the Corinthian believers in 1 Corinthians 6:9-11:

> Do you not know that the wicked will not inherit the kingdom of God? Do not be deceived: Neither the sexually immoral nor idolaters nor adulterers nor male prostitutes nor homosexual offenders nor thieves nor the greedy nor drunkards nor slanderers nor swindlers will inherit the kingdom of God. And that is what some of you were. But you were washed, you were sanctified, you were justified in the name of the Lord Jesus Christ and by the Spirit of our God (NIV).

In spite of their sin, these about whom Paul wrote had been cleansed and set apart in Christ. They were justified. They were set free to live a new life in Christ. Justification provides incentive to live for Christ.

Sanctification. Salvation encompasses the total life of the believer—past, present, and future. It may be viewed as three stages: as an instantaneous act, a continuing process, and a glorious consummation. The believer can say, "I have been saved" (see Rom. 10:9-10), "I am being saved" (see 1 Cor. 1:18), and "I will be saved" (see Rom. 13:11).

The initial stage of salvation is the instantaneous act of conversion. It is the experience of the new birth through faith in Christ, which is climaxed in justification. It may be described as having been saved from the penalty of sin. The penalty of sin has been lifted. The destiny of the believer is eternal life with the Father. The believer has passed from death to life. He will never be lost again (see John 5:24). He has been adopted into the family of God (see Rom. 8:15-23).

Unfortunately, many view salvation only in the sense of the initial act of redemption and conversion. When I was saved, the only emphasis I can recall is that I had been saved from sin and its penalty. I was filled with joy. I knew that I was not going to hell. I was going to heaven. But I was ignorant about my continuing life with Christ. I am sure that many new believers have the same type of experience I had.

No less emphasis should be placed on the initial experience of being saved. But much more emphasis and instruction must be given to living the continuing life of salvation, based on an understanding of what we have and who we are in Christ.

The second stage is the continuing process of salvation. It is the present tense of salvation. It is what the Scripture calls sanctification. The verb form in the New Testament is *hagiazo (to sanctify, set apart)*. The adjective is *hagios (holy)*, and the noun is *hagiasmos (holiness, sanctification)*. This process is expressed in the statement "I am being saved from the power of sin." "The message of the cross is foolishness to those who are perishing, but to us who are being saved it is the power of God" (1 Cor. 1:18, NIV).

Justification speaks of how a person becomes a Christian. Sanctification speaks of the continued spiritual growth of the Christian's life. Sanctification is both an act and a process. As an act, it takes place at the time of the conversion experience (see 1 Cor. 6:11). It is the act of God in setting apart and making holy in Christ the person who has been saved. It is not sinless perfection. The believer will not be made sinless until the final stage of salvation, when he is delivered from the presence of sin into the immediate, eternal presence of God. However, in God's sight, because of his justification and sanctification in union with Christ, God sees him as perfect. The believer is "accepted in the beloved" (Eph. 1:6). He is perfect in position before God but not in his life. He continues to struggle in the conflict with the power of sin in life. He is engaged in spiritual warfare of the Spirit against the flesh (see Gal. 5:16-20).

As a process, sanctification continues as a dynamic experience of growth in Christ throughout the believer's life. Salvation begins with the immediate, instantaneous act of being delivered from the penalty of sin. It continues with the process of being delivered by God's power from the power of sin in life: "Grow in the grace and knowledge of our Lord and Savior Jesus Christ" (2 Pet. 3:18, NIV). Growth is the normal result of salvation. It is commanded by God. Salvation is not a license for loose living (see Rom. 6). It is the liberation of Christ to enable the saved to become like Him. Liberty in Christ must not be seen as an "occasion to the flesh" (Gal. 5:13).

Christlikeness is God's purpose for the Christian's life. Paul wrote about the continuing experience of salvation: "Then we will no longer be infants, tossed back and forth by the waves, and blown here and there by every wind of teaching and by the cunning and craftiness of men in their deceitful scheming. Instead, speaking the truth in love, we will in all things grow up into him who is the Head, that is, Christ" (Eph. 4:14-15, NIV).

The Christian is to become like Him who lives within. God has made you holy in Christ. Therefore, be holy. Become what you are! Peter exhorted believers: "Prepare your minds for action; be self-controlled; set your hope fully on the grace to be given when Jesus Christ is revealed. As obedient children, do not conform to the evil desires you had when you lived in ignorance. But just as he who called you is holy, so be holy in all you do; for it is written: 'Be holy, because I am holy'" (1 Pet. 1:13-16, NIV).

The Christian's life is to be lived in obedient fellowship with God as a child of the Father. In doing so, he will be found faithful when Jesus comes in His glory.

Glorification. The final stage of salvation is glorious consummation. This final and future stage is called glorification. The expectancy of the completion of salvation is reflected in Romans 13:11: "This do, understanding the present time. The hour has come for you to wake up from your slumber, because our salvation is nearer now than when we first believed" (NIV).

God's ultimate purpose in salvation is to deliver the believer from the presence of sin into His eternal presence. The Christian is able to say, "I will be saved from the presence of sin." In the presence of God the power of sin will finally be broken. Full victory belongs to the Christian as he lives and reigns with Christ. Satan will be finally and completely put down: "The accuser of our brothers, who accuses them before our God day and night, has been hurled down" (Rev. 12:10, NIV).

Paul strongly emphasized what theologians call eschatological salvation, focusing on the second coming of Christ. The Christian should engage his life daily in eschatological living, living with the expectancy of our Lord's return, living each day as if it were the last. Paul comforted and encouraged the child of God in Romans 8:18: "I consider that our present sufferings are not worth comparing with the glory that will be revealed in us" (NIV).

The trials and temptations of this life are severe for the child of God. But he is not left to his own ability to keep himself saved until he is present with Christ: "Being confident of this, that he who began a good work in you will carry it on to completion until the day of Christ Jesus" (Phil. 1:6, NIV). Peter reiterated the truth that the believer is "kept by the power of God" for a salvation ready to be revealed at the last time (1 Pet. 1:5). The child of God is kept by the Lord Himself until he is present with the Lord. The glorious destiny of the saved will be considered in more detail later in this study. For now it suffices to say that the new birth provides salvation from start to finish, from the moment the believer trusts in Jesus until the time when the believer is with the Lord forever.

P E R S O N A L   L E A R N I N G   A C T I V I T Y   14

Review the section "Sanctification." On the lines below or on another sheet of paper write two or three sentences that describe what you believe *sanctification* means.

_____

_____

_____

_____

_____

_____

The New Birth: Results in Life

The life of the person who has been born again is characterized by change. Evidence of the new birth is present in the believer's heart and life. Jesus said that a good tree bears good fruit (see Matt. 7:17). First John gives several evidences of a genuine new-birth experience.

First, the born-again person walks in righteousness: "If you know that he is righteous, you know that everyone who does what is right is born of him" (1 John 2:29, NIV). He walks in the light (see 1 John 1:6-7). He obeys the commandments of the Lord (see 1 John 2:3). The hymn "Trust and Obey" expresses this great truth.

Second, the born-again person will not continue to practice sin: "No one who is born of God will continue to sin, because God's seed remains in him; he cannot go on sinning, because he has been born of God" (1 John 3:9, NIV). This statement does not mean that a Christian never sins. First John 1:8 declares that inevitably a Christian sins. Instead, it means that a born-again person will not go on living in deliberate, willful, premeditated sin. God has delivered the believer from that life.

Third, the born-again person loves the people of God: "We know that we have passed from death to life, because we love our brothers. Anyone who does not love remains in death" (1 John 3:14, NIV). A Christian cannot go on living with hatred and bitterness toward others. The sin of bitterness infects the individual's life and the church. No one sins in isolation. Churches grow weak and die from the lack of love. Christians are recognized as His disciples because they love one another (see John 13:35).

Fourth, the born-again person, believing that Jesus is the Christ, is committed to Him: "Everyone who believes that Jesus is the Christ is born of God" (1 John 5:1, NIV). The evidence of a true faith commitment to Jesus as the Christ is a clear indication of the reality of the new birth. This teaching pertains to the lordship of Christ. He is Lord. Those who are born in Him live under His lordship.

Fifth, the born-again person overcomes the world: "Everyone born of God overcomes the world. This is the victory that has overcome the world, even our faith" (1 John 5:4, NIV). Christians are in the world but not of the world. The world and its systems, pleasures, and philosophies are in opposition to Christ. The person who is born again finds the power through the Spirit, who abides in him and is greater than the one who is in the world, to live in victory over the world (see 1 John 4:4). The believer is not conformed to the world but transformed by the renewing of the mind (see Rom. 12:2).

Sixth, the born-again person has the witness of the Spirit in him that he is a child of God: "Anyone who believes in the Son of God has this testimony in his heart" (1 John 5:10, NIV). The Spirit witnesses to the spirit of the Christian to give assurance that he is saved and a part of God's family (see Rom. 8:16). Inner assurance marks the life of the Christian. The salvation of Christ is a know-so salvation.

Conclusion

Born again! It is the experience God has made available to "whosoever will" through the love gift of the death of His own Son: "God so loved the world, that he gave his only begotten Son, that whosoever believeth in him should not perish, but have everlasting life" (John 3:16). "As many as received him, to them gave he power to become the sons of God, even to them that believe on his name" (John 1:12).

DOCTRINE IN LIFE

The new birth is central to the experience of salvation. On a separate sheet of paper write your personal testimony. Try to limit yourself to one paragraph for each of the following topics.

1. What was your life like before you were born again?
2. How and when did you accept Jesus as Savior and Lord?
3. What difference is your experience of salvation making in your life today?

---

[1]Herschel H. Hobbs, *An Exposition of the Gospel of John* (Grand Rapids: Baker Book House, 1968), 79.
[2]Ibid., 80.

Salvation and Daily Living

QUESTIONS TO GUIDE YOUR STUDY
1. In what sense is salvation a process as well as an event?
2. What are some obstacles to growth in the Christian life?
3. What are the keys to growth and development in the Christian life?

Missionaries sometimes relate stories of being addressed as Jesus by people who have only recently been introduced to the gospel. One missionary was shocked when he heard someone say, "Here comes Jesus" and realized that the person was referring to him. At first the missionary thought that the comment was idolatrous. Then he realized that he was the representative of Jesus to that person. The missionary was Jesus to that person.

When Paul wrote to his beloved friends in Philippi, he admonished them to "continue to work out your salvation with fear and trembling" (Phil. 2:12, NIV). Then he assured them, "It is God who works in you to will and to act according to his good purpose" (Phil. 2:13). The truth of these verses is important. As God works in the heart of the redeemed person, He makes it possible for that person to live out the responsibilities of the Christian life in the world—to become the representative of Jesus in the world.

The name *Christian* probably means *like Christ.* The disciples were first called Christians at Antioch (see Acts 11:26). The name may not have been intended as a compliment by those who first used it. These early disciples were probably called Christians because they lived like Jesus Christ, spoke about Jesus, and were openly on mission for Him. Their lives were shining like lights in the world (see Phil. 2:15).

Living the Christ life faces the born-again person. How can anyone live like Jesus? It is difficult. No, it is impossible! Only Jesus can live like Jesus. The only possibility of living like Jesus is to allow Jesus to live His life through us.

Paul expressed the dilemma of his passionate desire but his inability to live the Christlike life when he said that what he desired to do, he did not, and what he did not want to do, he did (see Rom. 7:18-19). His conclusion followed: "What a wretched man I am! Who will rescue me from this body of death? Thanks be to God—through Jesus Christ our Lord" (Rom. 7:24-25, NIV). Jesus Christ is our only hope, not only for being saved but also for living the Christian life. Christ has come to dwell in the believer's life through faith (see Eph. 3:17). His indwelling presence is the enabling power for living the Christian life.

Salvation begins with the new birth. When conversion happens through repentance and faith, the believer is saved from the penalty of sin. This is justification through the sovereign act of God. The believer has peace with God (see Rom. 5:1).

When the believer is saved, she is not sinless. She is not perfect. This will happen when, either through death or when our Lord returns, God takes her to heaven. That will be glorification. Sin will no longer be a problem. She will be saved from the presence of sin.

The Christian's challenge is living the present life. The saved person is continuing to be saved from the power of sin in her life. This process is sanctification. The new life is a process of growing and maturing into the likeness of Christ. At conversion His *life* is within us, but His *likeness* is not within us. Sin still has a power over the believer, but sin's power is potentially broken through Christ's death and resurrection. Victory belongs to the Christian as she appropriates by faith all that is hers in Christ.

Salvation includes the entirety of the Christian's life. It is the *past act* of having been delivered from sin's penalty, the *present process* of being delivered from sin's power, and the *future prospect* of being delivered from sin's presence. Salvation from start to finish is the work of God in Christ.

Sometimes when Christian truth is presented, conversion is emphasized so much that converts receive the impression that turning to Christ from sin is all there is to the Christian life. J. B. Gambrell "once said that this was the end of the matter, but that it was the first end. Conversion is only the beginning of the Christian life. Nor is conversion the whole of salvation. Salvation includes everything that grows out of conversion, everything out to the resurrection."[1]

Salvation: A Process of Growth

A biblical understanding of salvation must include all of life, from the initial commitment of our lives to Jesus to the time when we are made perfect in His presence. This understanding of salvation necessitates an emphasis on growth in Christ. A Christian experience that focuses only on the initial decision a person makes to accept Christ is inadequate. This chapter will emphasize the ongoing nature of the Christian life. The biblical Christian is a growing Christian.

Sanctification. Biblically, sanctification is both an act and a process. It is God's divine transaction at conversion to set apart the believer for Himself and to make him holy in Christ. The foundation of sanctification is laid in the Old Testament in God's instruction to the Israelites to consecrate to Him the "firstborn, whatsoever openeth the womb . . . both of man and of beast" (Ex. 13:2). They also were told to consecrate the place where they were to meet with God (see Ex. 29:43), as well as the tabernacle and its furnishings (see Num. 7:1). These were set apart (sanctified) for the Lord and His use. Belshazzar (see Dan. 5) took the sanctified vessels of God from the temple in Jerusalem and misused them in a drunken orgy.

In the New Testament believers are called saints (sanctified, set-apart ones; see Rom. 1:7; 1 Cor. 1:2). The believer in Christ has been "sanctified through the offering of the body of Jesus Christ once for all" (Heb. 10:10; also see 1 Cor. 6:11). The believer has been sanctified, set apart, and made holy in Christ for God and His service. God has accomplished the act of sanctification in the believer, with the goal of working it out in the expression of his daily living.

Living the Christian life is a continuing process of growth. Sanctification is the ongoing experience of God at work in the believer's life: "May God himself, the God of peace, sanctify you through and through. May your whole spirit, soul and body be kept blameless at the coming of the Lord Jesus Christ. The one who calls you is faithful and he will do it" (1 Thess. 5:23-24, NIV). The Christian is often commanded to be holy in life, for he serves a God who is holy. The Christian life is one of struggle, to bring the life into conformity with the position God has given through the help of the Holy Spirit. Growth in Christ characterizes the Christian life.

God's purpose. The growing life is based on God's purpose in salvation. He is always at work through all things to conform the believer to the image of Christ: "We know that in all things God works for the good of those who love him, who have been called according to his purpose. For those God foreknew he also predestined to be conformed to the likeness of his Son" (Rom. 8:28-29, NIV). God does not cause all things. Many things happen to the believer as a result of sin in the world, of the actions of others, and of his own actions, which God does not cause. But the sovereign God works through all things, both good and bad, to bless His children and to benefit His kingdom. External circumstances are powerless to block God's purpose. He works through even the most difficult circumstances to fashion the Christian's life into Christ's image.

The Christian's attitude toward and response to circumstances determine their effect. God is always at work in the Christian's heart for spiritual growth: "It is God who works in you to will and to act according to his good purpose" (Phil. 2:13, NIV). By the indwelling Spirit God works to create the desire for His purpose. The Spirit ministers through life's circumstances to nurture the desire for His will in the lives of His people. If the believer resists the Spirit's leadership, God disciplines the believer. Through the difficult consequences created by resisting the Spirit's work, the believer is disciplined to confront his sinful attitude and to seek God's purpose. God disciplines His child to the extent necessary to get his attention.

Grace. By His grace God dynamically overshadows His child to produce growth. Grace demands discipleship. Jesus called His followers to a life of discipleship (see Matt. 16:24). A disciple is a learner and a follower of Christ. Dietrich Bonhoeffer called the theory of grace without discipleship "cheap grace." In cheap grace—

the world finds a cheap covering for its sins; no contrition is required, still less any real desire to be delivered from sin . . . the grace which amounts to the justification of sin without the justification of the repentant sinner who departs from sin and from whom sin departs. Cheap grace is not the kind of forgiveness of sin which frees us from the toils of sin. Cheap grace is the grace we bestow on ourselves. Cheap grace is the preaching of forgiveness without requiring repentance, baptism without church discipline, communion without confession, absolution without personal confession. Cheap grace is grace without discipleship, grace without the cross, grace without Jesus Christ, living and incarnate.[2]

Liberty. Does grace imply license, legalism, or liberty? Grace is not license for loose living, allowing one to continue in sin. Paul's preaching of grace was attacked at this point. He answered the attack in

Romans 6:1-2: "What shall we say, then? Shall we go on sinning so that grace may increase? By no means! We died to sin; how can we live in it any longer?" (NIV). Grace provides the means and incentive for overcoming sin.

The Christian does not begin saved by grace, then return to the legalism of human effort to grow. Legalism is not growth in grace. Emphasis placed on rule keeping brings the Christian into legalistic bondage that stifles growth. Paul exhorted the Galatians not to return to the bondage of legalism, from which Christ had set them free (see Gal. 3). Legalism and license are extremes at opposite ends of the pole of life.

The balanced Christian life is one of liberty. *Liberty* in Christ has freed the believer to live in the joy of the fellowship of obediently walking with Him. When the Spirit is Lord, there is liberty (see 2 Cor. 3:17). Living the growing Christian life involves the disciplines of Bible study, prayer, church attendance, witnessing, serving, and giving, but these disciplines should never become a rigid system of legalistic performance. In the same way, witnessing and soul winning are commands and duties of every Christian. But if they are reduced to merely performing a duty, a true witness can be hindered. The message of the gospel may be presented in a loveless spirit. A true witness is the overflow of the love and person of Christ, who lives within.

In *Classic Christianity* Bob George shares that such was his experience at one point in his life. He had begun his Christian life with a joy and a witness from the overflow. He had a great concern to reach the lost for Christ. He had a determination to lead people to Him. Bob studied much and learned techniques for effective soul winning. He grew in knowledge but not equally in spirit. Gradually, his joy, power, and fruitfulness diminished. He struggled within.

Then he said: "It seemed as if God was sending me a message: 'You used to share *Me* with people, Bob. Now you share your knowledge.' As I was becoming preoccupied with what I was learning about God's love and grace, though, I found myself excitedly sharing Christ again. And I started seeing the results again."[3]

Imagine a group of deaf and hearing people in a room. One man, listening to music, begins to tap his toes and snap his fingers rhythmically. A deaf man observes him and begins to tap his toes and snap his fingers, although he cannot hear. "After a little practice, the deaf man is snapping and tapping in time with the first man. He even smiles a little and shrugs: 'It's not *that* much fun,' he thinks, 'but it's okay.' "[4]

A third person observes. What does he see? Two men apparently doing the same thing. But there is a difference—all the difference in the world! The first man's actions are natural responses to the music he hears. The deaf person is only imitating outward actions, although he cannot hear a note. That is the difference between real Christianity, lived in the liberty of the Spirit, and legalism.[5]

PERSONAL LEARNING ACTIVITY 15

The author writes that a disciple is a learner and a follower. Define these words in terms of your personal discipleship.

Learner: _____

_____

_____

_____

Follower: _____

_____

_____

_____

Salvation: Obstacles to Growth

Growth in Christ as a disciple is not an option. It is essential as a natural outgrowth of the new-birth experience. Growth is the normal process for all living things. It is normal for animal life and for plant life. It is also normal for spiritual life. Nongrowth is abnormal. It is serious when a person does not grow and develop physically and mentally. Sadder still is the life of a person who has been a Christian for 10, 20, or 40 years yet is still a babe in Christ. God intends for His children to grow. He has provided all that is needed for their life and growth: "His divine power has given us everything we need for life and godliness through our knowledge of him who called us by his own glory and goodness. Through these he has given us his very great and precious promises, so that through them you may participate in the divine nature and escape the corruption in the world caused by evil desires" (2 Pet. 1:3-4, NIV). Because of the provision and promises of God the Christian is enabled and commanded to add to his faith the qualities that characterize spiritual growth (see 2 Pet. 1:5-8). He has the availability of the indwelling Holy Spirit to live a Spirit-filled, Spirit-directed life. When the Spirit is in control, He will bring forth His fruit of love, joy, peace, patience, kindness, goodness, faithfulness, gentleness, and self-control (see Gal. 5:22).

What, then, keeps a Christian from growing in Christ? What causes one who has new life within and every provision for his growth not to grow?

Spiritual ignorance. A primary factor in hindering the Christian's growth is spiritual ignorance. One may be saved yet, as a babe in Christ, not understand God's purpose for growth. A person may be in Christ yet not realize who he is in Christ and what he has in Christ. He may be ignorant that he has an old nature with which to contend, as well as a new nature that operates within him. He may be ignorant that the Christian life is warfare with a real spiritual enemy, the devil.

In the Great Commission our Lord charged the church not only to make disciples and baptize them but also to continue to teach them all things that He had commanded (see Matt. 28:19-20). When a baby is born, the parents do not cast the little one onto the street and say: "OK, Kid, you are born. We have done our part. Now you live it." Rather, they feed, nurture, and care for the child as she grows. Similarly, the church must provide the tender, nurturing, loving care of instructing the little ones in Christ, encouraging and training them in living the Christian life. Every life needs an encourager. Paul had Barnabas, who stood with him and helped enable him (see Acts 9:27). Everyone, like Paul, needs a Barnabas.

Growth involves realizing the finished work of Christ. At the cross the sin debt was paid once for all, and Satan was defeated. Sin and Satan have no authority over the believer. The believer is free to live for Christ as she realizes His finished work and claims His power over Satan.

Failure to identify the enemy. Growth involves identifying the enemy. The Christian has an enemy. Who is our enemy? God? God is not the Christian's enemy! Then why do we act as if God is the enemy, disobeying Him and His Word? God loves His child. He knows what is best for His child and has a high and holy purpose for him. God has already given us His highest and best in His Son. Surely, He will not withhold a lesser thing from us: "He who did not spare his own Son, but gave him up for us all—how will he not also, along with him, graciously give us all things?" (Rom. 8:32, NIV).

God is not the enemy. He is the source of victory. Trust Him. Obey Him. Faith in Him is victory. The enemy to be recognized and reckoned with is Satan.

Temptation to sin comes to the believer's life, but it does not come from God: "God cannot be tempted by evil, nor does he tempt anyone" (Jas. 1:13, NIV). But God permits temptation. He does not build a hedge around the believer to exempt him from facing a real world that is rampant with sin and the devil's activity. God permits temptation to test the believer so that, by faith, he may overcome the old tendencies toward sin: "No temptation has seized you except what is common to man. And God is faithful; he will not let you be tempted beyond what you can bear. But when you are tempted, he will also provide a way out so you can stand up under it" (1 Cor. 10:13, NIV).

God is faithful. You can trust Him. He screens every temptation to make sure that it is not more than the believer can bear. He always provides a way of escape so the believer can overcome. When the believer is victorious, he is strengthened for the next battle. Growth has taken place in the believer.

Who is the enemy? The devil is the real enemy. He is subtle and scheming. He seeks to outwit the child of God (see 2 Cor. 2:10-11). He masquerades as an angel of light (see 2 Cor. 11:14), subtly attacking the believer in the spiritual warfare of life. The devil is not omniscient, but he is smart. He knows the believer's weaknesses. He directs his temptations like "fiery darts" (Eph. 6:16) toward the believer's points of vulnerability. He knows just the target at which to aim his arrows of temptation. This is why the Word of God admonishes: "Love not the world, neither the things that are in the world. If any man love the world, the love of the Father is not in him. For all that is in the world, the lust of the flesh, and the lust of the eyes, and the pride of life, is not of the Father, but is of the world" (1 John 2:15-16).

The devil uses this world and its allurement to appeal to the believer's old, sinful nature. He uses the same threefold appeal with which he tempted Eve in the garden and confronted Jesus on the mountain, appealing to "the lust of the flesh," that is, to the sensual, fleshly desires in the old nature. He appeals to "the lust of the eyes" by placing deceitful, sinful images before a person to suggest sinful imaginations and fantasies. And he appeals to human pride to lead one to go his own way instead of God's way. But Satan has no authority over the believer. The victory has been won by our Lord!

A dear, older Christian woman said: "I have learned how to deal with Satan. When Satan knocks on my door, I look to see who is there. I send Jesus to the door, and Jesus says, 'Satan, you are at the wrong door.'" "The accuser of our brothers, who accuses them before our God day and night, has been hurled down. They overcame him by the blood of the Lamb and by the word of their testimony; they did not love their lives so much as to shrink from death" (Rev. 12:10-11, NIV). Believers overcome "by the blood of the Lamb." Satan was defeated at the cross by the blood of Christ. Believers may claim the authority and power of the blood over Satan. Believers overcome by their testimonies. They should continue to testify openly to the lordship of Christ. Believers overcome by not loving life so much that they are unwilling to die for Christ if necessary. Christians should love Jesus more than life itself. Such attitudes require growth in understanding the lordship of Christ. These attitudes bring victory to the Christian's life.

Failure to confront the old nature. Growth involves confronting the old nature, to which Satan appeals in his allurements. Satan has the power only to present the enticement to sin. He has no power to force the Christian to sin: "Each one is tempted when, by his own evil desire, he is dragged away and enticed. Then, after desire has conceived, it gives birth to sin; and sin, when it is full-grown, gives birth to death" (Jas. 1:14-15, NIV).

Satan is like a fisher who carefully and selectively baits the hook with just the right bait to lure the fish. But it is the fish that takes the bait. A person's desire for the bait causes him to reach out and take the bait. The old, sinful nature, which still resides within, wars to cause evil desire to arise and reach out for the bait. The old nature must be confronted. Paul identified it as the sinful nature (see Rom. 7:18,25, NIV; Gal. 5:16-17, NIV) and the old self (see Eph. 4:22, NIV).

PERSONAL LEARNING ACTIVITY 16

List the area or areas in which, as a believer, you struggle most with your old, sinful nature. Pray for God's help in the areas you identify.

Salvation: Keys to Christian Living

When a person is saved, he gains new life in Christ, with all its potential. The Spirit of God lives within, but the old self or sinful nature has not been eradicated. The believer still has in his life old patterns of thinking and acting that must be broken and old tendencies that must be overcome. The question is, How can one deal with the old nature? Paul instructed believers in Ephesians 4:22-24 to do three things: "to put off your old self, which is being corrupted by its deceitful desires; to be made new in the attitude of your minds; and to put on the new self, created to be like God in true righteousness and holiness" (NIV).

Affirming the new nature. The old nature cannot be stopped by mere human resolve. The negative behavior and attitudes must be replaced by positive behavior and attitudes. Paul illustrated this point practically in his instruction to replace lying with speaking the truth in love (see Eph. 4:25), to replace anger with forgiveness (see Eph. 4:26,31-32), and to replace stealing with working in order to have something to give (see Eph. 4:28).

The believer cannot overcome the old, sinful nature in his own strength. The renewing of the mind through the power of the Holy Spirit enables us to achieve victory. Paul testified to his own struggle and instructed believers to reckon or to "count yourselves dead to sin but alive to God in Christ Jesus" (Rom. 6:11, NIV). He shared his experience in Galatians 2:20: "I have been crucified with Christ and I no longer live, but Christ lives in me. The life I live in the body, I live by faith in the Son of God, who loved me and gave himself for me" (NIV).

The mind is renewed as one daily lives the crucified life under Christ's lordship. Paul said, "I die daily" (1 Cor. 15:31). It is effected by the Holy Spirit's convicting the believer of disobedience and calling her to repentance, confession of sin, and obedience. It is nurtured by the Holy Spirit through the Word of God so that resurrection power can be experienced in daily living.

The mind is the battleground on which the believer encounters Satan's attacks. He makes subtle suggestions to the believer's imagination in much the same fashion he did to Eve in the first temptation in

Genesis 3. If the believer entertains these suggestions, he will allow Satan to gain a stronghold, a base of operation, in his life. From such a base, Satan can influence the entire life for evil. The weapons with which to counter this attack are not worldly but divine power to demolish imaginations and strongholds by taking captive every thought and making it obedient to Christ (see 2 Cor. 10:4-5). The divine power is that of the Holy Spirit, working through the Word of God to guide the believer's mind in a thought life of obedience to Christ. It is imperative that the mind be permeated with the Word of God. The believer's mind is purified and fortified by the Word. He must know the Word. In our Lord's great prayer for His followers Jesus prayed to the Father, " 'Sanctify them by the truth; your word is truth' " (John 17:17, NIV). To realize truth liberates. When one acts on the basis of erroneous belief, he is in bondage. He cannot relate correctly to God, to others, or to circumstances. But when he knows and understands God's truth, he is freed to relate correctly and meaningfully: " 'You will know the truth, and the truth will set you free' " (John 8:32, NIV).

L. E. Maxwell tells the story of an old missionary who had long lived a defeated Christian life. "In his despair his eyes fell upon the words, 'Christ liveth in me.' 'What,' he said, 'is Christ actually living in me?' He jumped up,—solid Presbyterian though he was,—and danced round and round his table, saying, 'Christ liveth in me! Christ liveth in me!' When he realized that he was actually indwelt by the Crucified One, he came into blessed emancipation from the old self-life."[6]

Affirming fellowship with the Father. Growth involves the Christian in recognizing his relationship with the Father. The relationship never changes. It is unchanging because it depends on the faithfulness of the Father to the child. The relationship depends not on the ability of the child to cling to the Father but on the ability of the Father to hold on to the child. When disobedience comes into the life, the relationship is not affected. The relationship is permanent. However, the fellowship changes because it depends on the faithfulness of the child to the Father. When the child is unfaithful and disobedient to the Father, the fellowship is broken. Fellowship changes when sin enters a Christian's life, while the relationship remains constant.

When I was growing up on a cotton and cattle farm, Dad would assign my brother and me various chores. Occasionally, Dad would go to the nearby town to take care of business. He would leave us chores to do. When he came home, I could hear his pickup truck coming over the hill long before I could see it. My brother and I knew that he would have a bag of goodies for us. I would race to the road to meet him, that is, if I had done what he said. If I had not, I stayed in the barn. I did not want to be around him. I felt uncomfortable because I had not done what he said. Although he was still my father and the relationship had not changed, the fellowship had. He did not even know what I had done or had not done, but I wanted to avoid him. The problem was in me. I felt alienated until I admitted my disobedience, asked his forgiveness, and obeyed him.

Many Christians are defeated in life because they do not understand the distinction between fellowship and relationship. They become consumed with doubt, lose the assurance of salvation, and drift into spiritual depression. In such a state they become unfruitful and do not grow. Their spiritual energy is depleted. They cannot concentrate on living the Christian life because of their anxiety and loss of consciousness of the Lord's presence.

Celebrating security. The glorious Bible teaching of eternal security is a primary factor in the growth and daily living of the Christian life. The Bible teaches with certainty the doctrine of once saved, always saved. Those who teach a doctrine of falling from grace are teaching a doctrine of works salvation. Salvation, from start to finish, is by the grace of God. Celebrating this truth can fortify the believer in daily living.

The term *born again*, which Jesus used to describe the initial experience of salvation, substantiates the doctrine of eternal security. The term itself signifies permanence. When one is born, he never becomes unborn. Similarly, Paul said that the believer has "received the Spirit of adoption" (Rom. 8:15). Adoption under Roman law could never be reversed. The adopted child had all debts canceled and received all rights, privileges, and responsibilities of the natural son. The adopted son could never be disinherited. He was a coheir in the family. Thus, he was not subject to change. Scripture after Scripture affirms the doctrine of the eternal security of the believer. John 3:16 says, " 'Whoever believes in him shall not perish but have eternal life' " (NIV). The believer's life is eternal and everlasting. John 3:36 says that the believer has (present tense) eternal life. " 'He that . . . believeth on him that sent me, hath everlasting life, and shall not come into condemnation; but is passed from death unto life' " (John 5:24). Three positive affirmations are made about the person who hears the Word of Jesus and believes in the Father: (1) He has everlasting life. (2) He shall not come into condemnation. (3) He has passed from death to life.

In John 10:27-29 Jesus said that He gives to His sheep eternal life and that they shall never perish. The word *never* is emphatic in the Greek construction. No one can pluck them out of His hand.

God will complete the work of salvation that He has begun: "Being confident of this very thing, that he which hath begun a good work in you will perform it until the day of Jesus Christ" (Phil.1:6). Christ is able to keep that which has been committed to Him (see 2 Tim. 1:12). The child of God is kept by the power of God (see 1 Pet. 1:3-5). Nothing can separate the Christian from the love of Christ (see Rom. 8:35-39). The Holy Spirit, imparted to the believer, is God's guarantee of eternal life (see Eph. 1:13).

Eternal security is based on what has been called the doctrine of perseverance of the saints, meaning that the regenerate person continues in faith. "It is of the very nature of faith to persist. If it does not persist, it is not a living faith; it is merely an intellectual opinion, or a passing emotion or an empty profession."[7]

The denial of the truth of eternal security has as its source a disregard of biblical revelation and an attempt to humanize God. When someone rejects the truth of the Bible, he attributes human standards to God, rationalizing that if he were God, he would condemn the Christian who sins. But God is not human. He does not act as a person would act. God acts consistently with His own nature.

Dealing with sin. Inevitably, the questions come: If a saved person is not lost again when he sins, what happens? Does God allow the Christian to sin with no consequences?

Three things happen when a Christian sins: (1) He is chastened or disciplined for his sin (see Heb. 12:6-11; Ps. 89:26-34). Like an earthly father who loves his children, God disciplines to correct His disobedient children. All of the Christian's chastisement for sin will be here on this earth, not in eternity. (2) He loses the joy of his salvation (see Ps. 51:12). David was a child of God. He committed adultery and murder. His spirit was in turmoil and depression (see Ps. 32). He lost the joy of salvation but not salvation itself. Through the discipline of the Father he confessed his sin in repentance and rededication to God. (3) He loses the reward he might have had (see 1 Cor. 3:12). The person is saved, but the works are burned with fire. The true Christian cannot get by with sin. The backslider is the most miserable creature on earth. The Christian who is outside fellowship with Christ and His church is like a fish out of water. He cannot find satisfaction.

When fellowship with the Father is broken, it can be restored. One key to growth and living the Christian life is to understand the principle of how broken fellowship is restored.

God's intention is for His child to live in intimate, continuing fellowship with Him. To know the joy of that intimacy, we must walk in obedience moment by moment. When we sin, we must not continue in it. In repentance we must confess it, forsake it, and go on in obedience to the Father.

First John 1 describes the way of fullness of joy through fellowship with God and with others in the family of God: "If we walk in the light, as he is in the light, we have fellowship one with another, and the blood of Jesus Christ his Son cleanseth us from all sin" (1 John 1:7). The thrust of the present-tense verb is that His blood keeps on cleansing us. A Christian does sin: "If we say that we have no sin, we deceive ourselves, and the truth is not in us" (1 John 1:8). The indwelling Holy Spirit makes the Christian aware of his sin so he can confess it. When a Christian sins, the Holy Spirit is grieved (see Eph. 4:30-32). The Spirit communicates His grief to the spirit of His sinning child. Sin is foreign and out of place in the heart of a born-again child of God. The presence of unholiness in the holy vessel of a life inhabited by the Holy Spirit creates inner conflict and tension. As has been stated earlier, God chastens his child to bring correction. God chastens through whatever measure is required to bring correction (see Heb. 12:6-11).

Sin in a Christian's life produces pain. It is a foreign substance. Pain alerts the Christian to the presence of sin so he will confess it and ask God to remove it. It is much like the person who gets a speck of steel in his eye. If it goes unattended, it penetrates deeper, and the person risks blindness. Everything in the person's body reacts to attempts to remove it. It is painful. Pain is a God-given alert system. First, the eye closes for protection. Then the tear ducts attempt to wash it out. The hand automatically moves to attempt to get it out. If that does not work, the mouth calls for help. The feet go into action, taking the person to the doctor to have the object removed.

Similarly, a Christian's whole being reacts to the presence of sin and its misery. Yet the old, sinful nature resists confessing sin. The human tendency is toward self-protection. The tendency is to minimize, whitewash, justify, or rationalize sin. The favorite technique of defensiveness is to blame it on someone else, a common practice since Adam blamed Eve and Eve blamed Satan.

Only God's way is effective in dealing with sin in the Christian's life: "If we confess our sins, he is faithful and just to forgive us our sins, and to cleanse us from all unrighteousness" (1 John 1:9). Confessing is more than simply admitting our sin. The Greek word for *confess* is *homologeo*. It means *to confess, agree with,* or *say the same thing as*. The prefix *homo* means *the same as* or *alike*. *Logos* means *word* or *expression*. Confession of sin, then, means to say the same thing God says about our sin—to agree with God about it—and to identify it as God identifies it. Confession involves the internal response of repudiating the sin. Confessing sin is specific, identifying the sin as God identifies it and renouncing it. Confession is the human part; yet even this is stimulated by the Holy Spirit. God's part is to forgive and cleanse.

What does God do when we confess our sin? First, God forgives when we confess. The New Testament word for *forgive* is *aphiemi*. It can be translated as *let go, send away, forgive, cancel,* or *pardon*. Many days as a boy in the hot summertime I watched the fluffy, white clouds and imagined what they resembled as they became different shapes. Gradually, a cloud would dissipate. Soon it would be gone as it dispersed in the sky. God's forgiveness of the confessing Christian's sin is like that. He cancels the sin. It is no longer there, as far as God is concerned.

God cleanses the heart and mind as we confess our sins. The Greek word is *katharidzo*. Literally, it means *to cleanse, purify,* or *set free*. The word indicates that as we confess our sin, God acts within us to cleanse, purify, and remove it. Two English words are derived from the word *katharidzo*. The medical term *catheterize* is the process of removing impurities from a body. The second, *catharsis*, is a psychological term. It means *to vent pent-up emotions so that release and relief are achieved*. When God cleanses, He removes the spiritual impurities from our lives so that we can experience healing and victory.

Confession has two dimensions, vertical and horizontal. The circle of the confession should include the circle of the offense. If the sin is private, the confession should be private between the individual and God. If the sin is against God and others, the confession should include those who have been wronged in order to restore fellowship (see Matt. 5:23-24).

One morning I was leaving my office to keep an appointment. At the door I met a very distraught woman whom I didn't know, carrying a bag of clothing. I asked if I could help. She said she was bringing clothes for our benevolence ministry. I told her that I would call my secretary, who would receive them. When she appeared disappointed, I realized that the bag of clothes was merely a means to come through the door to find someone who could help her. I asked again, "Is there something I can do?"

Brokenly, she answered: "May I talk to you? I am so troubled." She came into my office and began to pour out her hurt. She said: "I do not want to live. I am thinking about suicide."

As we talked, I told her that often two things in the spiritual life contribute to such feelings, guilt and hostility. She said that as a Christian, she was not aware of a particular sin in her life that would produce such guilt feelings. Then I asked if she had hostility, anger, or bitterness toward any person. She began to weep as she cried: "I hate her! Ten years ago she took my husband. I have hated her for all these years!"

We discussed the fact that the sins of her husband and of the other woman were their own but that her reaction of bitterness belonged to her. She was responsible for it. As we studied 1 John 1, she said that she would like to pray and confess her sin to God. Her prayer went something like this: "O God, for 10 years I have hated her. Please forgive me and cleanse me. Help me to forgive, love, and reach out to her in love."

When she concluded her prayer, she looked up at me with a new light in her eyes and a smile on her face. She said: "For the first time in 10 years I have peace in my heart. I am ready to go on living!"

In spite of what others had done, she had victory, and fellowship with God had been restored.

To live in victory, it is important that sin be confessed immediately after it has been committed. When sin is committed, the Holy Spirit convicts and creates awareness. Instantaneous confession should be the practice of the Christian, wherever he is. He should then claim the fullness and control of the Holy Spirit and obey Him.

Growth always involves the work of the Holy Spirit in the believer. He convicts of sin. He leads and guides the believer (see Rom. 8:14). He enables and empowers the believer in living the Christian life and for witnessing and ministry.

Following God's will. Living a growing Christian life involves knowing and doing the will of God: "Be not conformed to this world: but be ye transformed by the renewing of your mind, that ye may prove what is that good, and acceptable, and perfect, will of God" (Rom. 12:2). Here are three characteristics of the will of God. The will of God is good. It is the best way for the Christian. God is omniscient. He knows all things. He wants what is best for His child. God's will is good for the one who does it and for all who are related to him.

God's will is acceptable, or well pleasing. It fits just right. When a woman buys a dress, if it does not fit right, she is uncomfortable in it and does not want to wear it. If it is tailored to fit, she wears it with ease. God's will is "tailor-made" to fit the Christian.

God's will is perfect. This does not suggest that the one who does God's will is sinless. Instead, it means that God's will is complete. It always leads to the right point and place.

God's will is to be lived in practical, everyday living. To do His will, one must know what it is. Four basic principles are involved in discerning it. First, knowing the will of God involves the Word of God. The Scriptures instruct the believer in what is right (see 2 Tim. 3:16-17). They equip the Christian to do His will. God never leads His child to do anything that is not consistent with His Word. Second, knowing God's will involves the leadership of the Holy Spirit. The Spirit gives inner impressions as He guides the believer. However, not every impression comes from the Holy Spirit. We are to "try the spirits whether they are of God" (1 John 4:1). An impression should be put to the Scripture test: Is it consistent with the principles of the Scripture? It should be put to the morality test: Is it moral? Put it to the evangelistic test: Will it result in a positive witness for Christ? Wait on the Lord to confirm the impression. Third, knowing the will of God involves circumstances or open doors. If God wills a certain thing, He will open doors to provide circumstances that make it possible. It is appropriate to try the doors. If the door remains closed, it is evident that this is not God's will or that the time is not right. Fourth, knowing the will of God involves the sound-mind principle: "God hath not given us the spirit of fear; but of power, and of love, and of a sound mind" (2 Tim. 1:7). It is conviction based on reason. God gave us a mind with which to think and reason. Gather and assimilate the facts and data about the situation.

Utilizing these four principles aids the believer in knowing God's will. But the major factor in knowing it is a willingness to do it. Surrendering to God opens the life for God to reveal His will. Paul exhorts believers to "present your bodies a living sacrifice, holy, acceptable unto God" (Rom. 12:1) to prove His will. As a Christian walks in obedience to Christ and does the will of God, she continues to grow in Christlikeness.

Living as disciples. Living a growing Christian life requires discipline. Jesus called His followers disciples. That designation suggests a life-style. The discipline of a Christian life begins with the internal self-discipline of yielding to the Holy Spirit's control. Paul spoke of his internal self-discipline: "I keep under my body, and bring it into subjection: lest that by any means, when I have preached to others, I myself should be a castaway" (1 Cor. 9:27). Such an attitude causes a believer to incorporate activities into his life that are conducive to growth.

Conclusion

Living the life that has been given to us in our salvation experience involves growth. Healthy growth makes "you that ye shall neither be barren nor unfruitful in the knowledge of our Lord Jesus Christ" (2 Pet. 1:8). This chapter has said much about this growth. In summary, five disciplines are necessary for balanced, consistent nurture of a healthy, growing Christian life.

The Bible. The Word of God nourishes God's child, providing milk for the babes in Christ (see 1 Pet. 2:2) and meat for the more mature (see 1 Cor. 3:1-3). It gives promises, commands, instruction, and guidance for the Christian. It is profitable or useful for doctrine—to teach us how to live; for reproof—to show us if, when, and how we are wrong; for correction—to stand us up straight and put us right; and for instruction in righteousness—to guide us in successful living (see 2 Tim. 3:16).

The Christian should read the Bible daily, study it diligently, hear it regularly, memorize it consistently, and meditate on it continuously. The psalmist said,

> I have hidden your word in my heart
> that I might not sin against you (Ps. 119:11, NIV).

The Word of God changes lives.

Prayer. Prayer is necessary for the growing life in Christ. Prayer changes things. Among the things that prayer changes are the heart and life of the one who prays. Daily times of prayer, incorporated with Bible reading, should be set aside in devotion to Christ. In a spirit and an attitude of prayer the believer is to "pray without ceasing" (1 Thess. 5:17). An acronym to guide a Christian's prayer life is ACTS:

A Adoration. Worship and praise God.

C Confession of sin and wrong.

T Thanksgiving in everything.

S Supplication to God for one's needs and those of others. Intercession for others should be a daily practice.
Surrender to God's will.
Silence, listening for God to speak.

Fellowship. Fellowship with believers is necessary for growth in Christ. Every Christian needs the fellowship of others in corporate worship and Bible study. In the body of Christ we are "members one of another" (Rom. 12:5). Christians are commanded to remain faithful in church attendance to stimulate one another to love and good works (see Heb. 10:23-25). We are to "bear . . . one another's burdens" (Gal. 6:2).

Witnessing and ministry. Witnessing and ministry to others for Christ are essential disciplines for growth, as well as fruitfulness, in life. Witnessing is every Christian's job (see Acts 1:8). Consistent witnessing keeps the life filled with vitality. It stimulates the Christian to Bible study, prayer, and consistent living. Caring ministry to others stimulates love for Christ and for people.

Stewardship. Faithful stewardship helps to keep the life growing. Tithing in obedience to the Scripture and giving beyond the tithe express trust in God, as well as growing the life in faith (see Mal. 3:8-11; 2 Cor. 9:6-15; Heb. 7:8). Giving confronts one of humanity's worst enemies, greed. Selfishness is overcome through giving. Trusting God for the necessities of life as one honestly and productively works to earn his livelihood opens the life for growth. The giver's life becomes a channel of blessing rather than a reservoir of selfishness.

These five disciplines are to be incorporated into life regularly. Yet they should not become legalistic routines. Growth occurs as they are practiced in the vitality of the Spirit.

Motivation for living and growing comes from living a Christ-centered life: "Set your affections on things above, not on things on the earth" (Col. 3:2). Paul gave an excellent motto for living for Christ with enthusiasm: "Whatsoever ye do, do it heartily, as to the Lord, and not unto men" (Col. 3:23). Whatever a Christian does, if it is worth doing, he is to do it with all his heart, with enthusiasm. To do so, he must do it "as to the Lord," putting Christ first and doing it in worship to and service for Him. If it is done only for people, the Christian will be unstable. At times people will not approve, assist, acclaim, or reward. If it is done for the Lord, the Christian will continue to grow and serve as long as the Holy Spirit directs.

Growth should never cease in the Christian life. Living the Christ-centered life is not completed until God takes the Christian home to heaven. God never retires his child from living for Christ, witnessing, and serving Him. When Paul was facing death, he said: "I have fought a good fight, I have finished my course, I have kept the faith" (2 Tim. 4:7).

A faithful Christian in his 80s, still faithfully witnessing and winning souls, has the following verse as his motto: "Now also when I am old and greyheaded, O God, forsake me not; until I have shewed thy strength unto this generation, and thy power to every one that is to come" (Ps. 71:18). Though his voice is not what it once was, he still sings praise to his Lord.

DOCTRINE IN LIFE

Choose one of the activities below to express your discipleship this week. If you prefer, substitute an activity that is more suitable for you.

1. Visit patients in a hospital or a nursing home.
2. Contact someone who has recently experienced bereavement or another problem. Offer encouragement and help.
3. Volunteer your time and services to a ministry in your church or community in which you do not usually participate.
4. Make a visit to witness to someone.
5. Other:_____

---

[1]W. T. Conner, *Gospel Doctrines* (Nashville: Sunday School Board of the Southern Baptist Convention, 1925), 101.

[2]Dietrich Bonhoeffer, *The Cost of Discipleship* (New York: Macmillan Company, 1949), 46-47. Used by permission.

[3]Bob George, *Classic Christianity* (Eugene, Oregon: Harvest House Publishers, Inc., 1989), 158. Used by permission.

[4]Ibid., 152-53.

[5]Adapted from George, 153.

[6]L. E. Maxwell, *Born Crucified* (Chicago: Moody Press, 1945), 17.

[7]Conner, 111.

Salvation and the Church

QUESTIONS TO GUIDE YOUR STUDY
1. *What does it mean to say that the church is God's called-out people?*
2. *In what sense is the church general (made up of all believers)? In what sense is the church local?*
3. *What does the Bible mean when it refers to the church as the body of Christ?*
4. *Why is the church important to the believer?*

Amazing! This is the word John Newton chose to describe God's grace in salvation. As a boy, he ran away to sea, then to Africa, where he was sold to an African woman. He sank so low that he lived only on crumbs from her table and wild yams dug at night. His clothing was reduced to a single shirt, which he washed in the ocean.

When he finally escaped, he went to the natives, accepting their base life. Later, he became the captain of a slave-trading vessel. He sank to the lowest depths of depravity. But the power of God, through the witness of a missionary, changed his life. He wrote these words:

> Amazing grace! how sweet the sound,
> That saved a wretch like me!
> I once was lost, but now am found,
> Was blind, but now I see.

This great hymn was Newton's testimony. Multitudes today sing it with joy as their own.

In a church in London that he pastored is the epitaph that Newton wrote for himself. It reads: "Sacred to the memory of John Newton, once a libertine and blasphemer and slave of slaves in Africa, but renewed, purified, pardoned, and appointed to preach that Gospel which he had laboured to destroy!"[1]

The conversion of John Newton well illustrates the amazing grace of God in an individual's salvation. It also illustrates God's design for the Christian's becoming a meaningful part of the body of Christ, His church. Salvation is an individual, personal relationship with our saving Lord. But the life of one who is saved cannot be lived in isolation.

In the beginning God created people to live in the fellowship of love, communication, and unity with Him and others. Human sin disrupted, distorted, and destroyed the relationship with God and others.

God purposed a new creation in Christ that would be to the praise of His glorious grace (see Eph. 1:6). The new creation is both individual and corporate. Individually, "we have redemption through his blood, the forgiveness of sins, in accordance with the riches of God's grace that he lavished on us with all wisdom and understanding" (Eph. 1:7-8, NIV). And corporately, "he made known to us the mystery of his will according to his good pleasure, which he purposed in Christ, to be put into effect when the times will have readied their fulfillment—to bring all things in heaven and on earth together under one head, even Christ" (Eph. 1:9-10, NIV).

In Christ and under His headship God has brought together those who were "separate from Christ, excluded from citizenship in Israel and foreigners to the covenants of promise, without hope and without God in the world" (Eph. 2:12, NIV). He has made the two (Jew and Gentile) one and has broken down the barrier of hostility: "His purpose was to create in himself one new man out of the two, thus making peace, and in this one body to reconcile both of them to God through the cross, by which he put to death their hostility" (Eph. 2:15-16, NIV).

God is building for Himself a people in this world. We refer to the people of God in the world as the church. The church is central in God's purpose for humankind. Its founder is the Lord Jesus Christ. As He instructed His apostles about His approaching death and about their counting the cost of discipleship, He revealed His great purpose: " 'On this rock I will build my church, and the gates of Hades will not overcome it' " (Matt. 16:18, NIV).

The Church: God's Called-out People

Jesus chose the word *ekklesia,* a compound Greek word made up of the preposition *ek (out of)* and the verb *kaleo (to be called)* for His church. The Greeks used the word to refer to a body of citizens who were called out and gathered to discuss the affairs of the town or state (see Acts 19:39). In the Septuagint it is used to designate the gathering of Israel, summoned for any definite purpose, or a gathering regarded as representative of the whole nation. Jesus used it to refer to His people, who are the called-out ones, called out from sin to salvation, from death to life, from hell to heaven, from slavery to Satan to service to the Savior, and from the bondage of spiritual darkness to the liberty of the Holy Spirit.

Today there is a building-centered mentality about church. A church uses buildings as a meeting place, but church is not a building made of wood or bricks. A church uses organization but is not merely an organization. It is common for people to think in terms of attending church, but church is not a meeting we attend. We may meet with the church when it gathers, but church is not another club or fraternity to which we allocate a segment of our time, money, and activity. All of these buildings, organizations, and activities are the externals of church life. Essentially, church is people—people called out by our Lord, people who have received their life from Jesus Christ, people who are sharing that life with one another, people who are extending the Christ-life to all those around them. Church is people sharing Jesus!

The church is all the people of God. The word *ekklesia (church)* is used 115 times in the New Testament. It is used in two senses, general and local. First, the general sense is used 20 times to refer to the total body of the redeemed, including every born-again person through all the ages of history. It includes the saved, regardless of race, nationality, culture, or denomination. It is the body of believers who will be caught up to meet the Lord when He comes again. In the general sense, there is one church. It is not an organization; it is an organism. It does not have organizational unity; it has spiritual unity. This spiritual unity of the church is the "profound mystery" of Christ and the church spoken of in Ephesians 5:32.

What a joy it is to meet a person, perhaps on the other side of the earth, and find a brother or sister in Christ. On an evangelistic trip to Korea, after flying all night, I went through customs. I had a supply of bilingual booklets presenting the gospel of Christ, written by Billy Graham. I knew that Graham had preached a great crusade in Seoul, in which millions of Koreans had gathered to hear him. I handed a booklet to the young Korean customs official and said: "Here is some material about Jesus Christ. Billy Graham wrote it. Have you heard him preach?"

The young man smiled broadly, reached out to shake my hand, and said, "I am a Christian also."

This man, the first person I met in Seoul, Korea, was a brother. The love and unity of Christ break through all barriers. His fellowship binds the church together as one body indwelled by our Lord. In heaven there will be one church with Christ the Head. That will be glory to sit together in heavenly places in the presence of Jesus Christ.

The church is a local body. Some have called the general church the invisible church. The general or invisible church was visibly expressed in local congregations at its inception in New Testament times. The word *church* is used 95 times in the local sense in the New Testament. Over 82 percent of the occurrences of the word *church* in the New Testament refer to local churches. The local church gives practical expression to Christ's teachings, carrying out His mission and ministry. In Revelation 2—3 Jesus gave John messages for the seven churches, local congregations of believers in Asia. Paul wrote to individual, local churches, for example, "to the church of God in Corinth" (1 Cor. 1:2, NIV). In Galatians 1:2, "to the churches in Galatia" (NIV), the word *churches* is plural, referring to numerous bodies of believers.

Years ago my pastor taught me a formal definition of *local church:* A local church is a body of baptized believers in Jesus Christ who have voluntarily banded together to carry out the commission of Christ.

Each word of the definition is meaningful. A church is a body drawn together by our Lord to Himself. It is a body of believers with faith commitments to Christ. They have voluntarily, without coercion by individuals, parents, or the state, banded together through their mutual faith and trust in the person of Jesus Christ.

They are baptized in Him. Their baptism is both spiritual and physical. Spiritually, they have been baptized by the Holy Spirit: "We were all baptized by one Spirit into one body" (1 Cor. 12:13, NIV). Every believer experiences the baptism of the Holy Spirit in the new birth. This baptism incorporates the believer into union with Christ and into unity with the body of Christ. Spiritual baptism is outwardly expressed through the physical act of water baptism. The immersion in water and the raising of the believer from the water symbolically declare faith in the death, burial, and resurrection of Christ, to whom he has committed his life. They testify to one's death to the old life of sin and resurrection by the power of God to new life to be lived for Christ. Through spiritual baptism one comes into the spiritual body of Christ. Through outward baptism in water one confesses faith in Jesus and becomes a part of a local body of believers to share in the fellowship of a local church.

Every believer should openly confess faith in Jesus Christ and should become a part of God's called-out ones in a local church. Secret discipleship is no discipleship at all. It is unthinkable that one should experience the saving, resurrection love and power of Christ without making this faith known through public profession and church membership. The faith of a Christian is to be openly, verbally confessed. The *ekklesia* of God, His called-out church, is the proper setting for believers to share their faith, unite in fellowship, discover their spiritual gifts, and prepare for their ministry in the world.

The church is on mission. The church, those called out by God, is on mission. The purpose of believers' coming together is to carry out the commission of Christ in His world. What Jesus came to do, He left His church to continue to accomplish. The commission of Christ is clear: " 'Go and make disciples of all nations, baptizing them in the name of the Father and of the Son and of the Holy Spirit, and teaching them to obey everything I have commanded you. And surely I am with you always, to the very end of the age' " (Matt. 28:19-20, NIV).

The mission of the church is to reach people and disciple them so they can reach other people and disciple them. This is the mission of Jesus. Consequently, this is the mission of a local church.

PERSONAL LEARNING ACTIVITY 17

The author defines *local church* as *a body of baptized believers in Jesus Christ who have voluntarily banded together to carry out the commission of Christ.* On the lines below or on another sheet of paper rewrite this definition in your own words.

_____

_____

_____

_____

_____

The Church: The Body of Christ

The church is the body of Christ: "He is the head of the body, the church; he is the beginning and the firstborn from among the dead, so that in everything he might have the supremacy" (Col. 1:18, NIV).

Indwelling power. Why is the analogy of a human body used to refer to the church? It vividly portrays the relationship between Christ and His church. Just as our bodies house us as persons, Christ comes to take up His residence in us, individually and collectively, through our faith. We are His body. He lives in us through His Spirit: "Do you not know that your body is a temple of the Holy Spirit, who is in you, whom you have received from God? You are not your own; you were bought at a price. Therefore honor God with your body" (1 Cor. 6:19-20, NIV).

What glorious potential this is! Here is the secret of power in the church. Paul expressed it in his prayer for a local church, the Ephesian believers: "For this reason I kneel before the Father, from whom his whole family in heaven and on earth derives its name. I pray that out of his glorious riches he may strengthen you with power through his Spirit in your inner being, so that Christ may dwell in your hearts through faith" (Eph. 3:14-17, NIV). God empowers the church, individually and corporately, with His mighty power through His Spirit by the indwelling of Christ.

The fact that Christ lives in us enables us to know that which is unknowable, His love that surpasses knowledge. The reality of being in Christ and Christ's being in us fills us with all the fullness of God (see Eph. 3:18-19). Ephesians 3:20 speaks of the power of the church. What is He able to do by His mighty power? He is able to do what we ask, not only what we ask but also all we ask, not only all we ask but also all we can imagine, not only all we can ask or imagine but also more than all we can ask or imagine, not only more than all we can ask or imagine but also immeasurably more than all we can ask or imagine. How is He able? "According to his power" (v. 20, NIV)! Where is He able to manifest such power? Not out there somewhere in the world or in the universe. His power "is at work within us" (v. 20, NIV) to bring glory to Him in the church. God is ready to work mightily in and through the church by the power of the indwelling Christ, to the praise of His glorious purpose.

The most exciting adventure on earth is to be a part of a dynamic local church, fulfilling the mission of Christ. In God's plan the local church is primary. Occasionally, someone points an accusing finger at the church and says: "I do not need the church. I believe in Christ. I love Jesus, but I have no use for the church." Such an attitude is contradictory. It cannot be true. One cannot deeply love Jesus without loving what He loved. Christ loved the church. He died for the church (see Eph. 5:25).

Experiencing Christ's work of salvation and His indwelling presence initiates a relationship between a believer and the church. Love and appreciation for the local church characterize the redeemed life. It is said of new believers, some of whom had been antagonistic toward the church, in Acts 2:41-47: "Those who accepted his [Peter's] message were baptized. . . . They devoted themselves to the apostles' teaching and to the fellowship, to the breaking of bread and to prayer. . . . They gave to anyone as he had need. Every day they continued to meet together . . . praising God and enjoying the favor of all the people. And the Lord added to their number daily those who were being saved" (NIV).

Gathered and scattered. Two perspectives of the life of a local church that is functioning as the body of Christ can be identified. First, it is the church gathered. Second, it is the church scattered. A church gathers for worship and scatters for witness. It gathers for instructing, equipping, fellowship, planning, and mutual support. It scatters for evangelism and ministry.

The gathered perspective is important for the spiritual life and preparation of members. On the Lord's Day and at other times, the church meets together. We are commanded not to forsake the assembling of ourselves together (see Heb. 10:25). Christ is present with His people in a special way as they come together in His name (see Matt. 18:20). Worship, fellowship, and growing together bring joy to Christians and glory to God.

The scattered perspective is equally important for the church. As the church scatters on Monday through Saturday, it is as truly the church as when it gathers on Sunday. In fact, its gathering together is less than what God would have it be if it does not result in daily, effective witness and ministry.

Throughout the week everywhere members go in the community and the world, they are the church indwelled by the living Christ. Through each member the Lord of the church reaches out to do again all He did when He was here in the flesh. He is here in us to love people, minister to people, and bring them to God. What tremendous potential this is! Even a small church can literally penetrate and transform its area as its members share Christ through their life-style and witness in neighborhoods, schools, plants, factories, offices, hospitals, and government. As a church understands and engages in the mission of Christ in ministry and evangelism in the marketplace, it becomes salt to the earth and light to the world (see Matt. 5:13-14). Every member is on mission for Christ in the marketplaces of life. When this happens, the radiance of the light of Christ will penetrate every sin-darkened stratum of a decadent world.

Let the church be the church gathered and scattered! Such was the church of the New Testament. Seemingly, the church in Jerusalem had become content with the narrow boundaries of its locality. It had not yet comprehended the world vision of its founder. With the stoning of Stephen, great persecution arose that scattered the church. All except the apostles were scattered through Judea and Samaria: "Those who had been scattered preached the word wherever they went" (Acts 8:4, NIV). The word for *preached* in verse 4, *euaggelitzomenoi*, means *evangelizing*. They went everywhere evangelizing with the Word. The word *scatter* suggests the general broadcasting of seed. Everywhere the life of a Christian was planted, it bore the fruit of faith as people were brought to saving knowledge of Christ. Through the witnessing life of the church God spread the gospel. Centuries have passed, but the mission of the church has not changed. Let the church be the church!

The Head of the church. The function of a local church is to be an expression of the body of Christ under the headship of Jesus. Under its Head the body maintains a balance of priority. The book *Total Church Life* presents the threefold priority of a church:

1. A church is to exalt the Savior. Christ is Head of the church, His body (see Col. 1:18). He is to have preeminence. We are to lift Him up.
2. The church is to equip the saints (see Eph. 4:11-12). The church, the called-out ones, must be equipped to live the Christ-life and to extend His life to others. When God's people are equipped, they will do the work of ministry and build up the body of Christ in maturity and in number.
3. The church is to evangelize the lost (see Acts 1:8). When Christ is exalted and the people of God are equipped for ministry, the church will reach the lost. Christ came to seek and to save that which was lost. If a church is His body, He lives within. His mission becomes our mission. As beats the heart of Jesus, so beats the heart of His body, the church. It will evangelize the sinner![2]

The vitality of a church flows from its body—life under its Head, the Lord Jesus Christ. He is Head of the church. Ephesians 1:18-23 declares this truth majestically:

> . . . that you may know . . . his uncomparably great power for us
> who believe. That power is like the working of his mighty
> strength, which he exerted in Christ when he raised him from the
> dead and seated him at his right hand in the heavenly realms, far
> above all rule and authority, power and dominion, and every title
> that can be given, not only in the present age but also in the one to
> come. And God placed all things under his feet and appointed
> him to be head over everything for the church, which is his body,
> the fullness of him who fills everything in every way (NIV).

The lordship of Christ over all creation and His headship over the
church have been established by His death, resurrection, ascension,
and indwelling the church in the person of the Holy Spirit. At the
consummation of this age He will come as Lord of lords and King of
kings. There is no place for discouragement as the church lives and
functions under His headship.

Paul wrote pointedly about the Head-body relationship of Christ
and the church in his Epistles to the Romans, Corinthians, Ephesians,
and Colossians. He focused on it particularly in 1 Corinthians 12,
comparing a church to a human body.

Unity is a primary characteristic of an effective church. Christ uni-
fies the church. Under its Head, the Lord Jesus, "the body is a unit,
though it is made up of many parts; and though all its parts are many,
they form one body. So it is with Christ" (1 Cor. 12:12, NIV). His
headship is an absolute. There cannot be two heads in the same body.
None can be His rival. Disruption of the fellowship of the body-life
results when anyone attempts to rival Jesus for headship. Humanly,
the church is a democracy; but spiritually, it is a theocracy. When a
church comes together in a business meeting to make decisions, members should not decide what they want, divide into sides, and wage a
campaign to get their way. The church should get on its knees, discern
in prayer the direction of its Head, and get up to vote His will in unity.
Christ is not divided. Division in the body does not reflect His
headship.

A church, like a human body, has only so much energy, strength,
and resources. If they are dissipated through contention, backbiting,
gossip, and fighting, there is none left to fulfill the mission of the
Head.

The Head has vision, sets the direction, coordinates the members, and supplies guidance for the body. No one but Jesus can bring unity in the body. Human personality and programs can be instrumental but cannot effect unity in the church. It is paramount that the church be Christ-centered. "Is Christ preeminent in this?" should be the overshadowing question in all the church does. He is both Lord and lifegiver of the church.

A local church is to be a visible expression of the spiritual body of Christ in a community. A Christ-filled local church body reflects the radiant glory of the person of the indwelling Christ. Every member is a vital part of a church's total life. Whatever a church is, it is the composite of all its members. A church member should never say, "I wonder why *they* did thus and so at the church." Church is not *they*. It is *we*! We are the church. By our actions, words, and attitudes, we make a local church what it is.

It must be remembered that a local church is composed of members who are indwelled by the divine Son of God yet who themselves are imperfect. Even the first church had human flaws. It had Judas, who betrayed the Lord; it had Simon Peter, who denied Him; it had Thomas, the doubter; it had Paul and Barnabas, who split up over taking Mark with them on a mission trip. But in spite of its human frailties, Christ nourishes and cherishes His church as His body (see Eph. 5:29). He continues to work in the church to develop Christlikeness within and to extend the Christ-life without.

Unity and diversity. Although the church is one body, it is made up of many members. No two are exactly alike. Diversity in the body is its dynamic. Every member is important. Everybody is somebody in the Lord's body: "If the ear should say, 'Because I am not an eye, I do not belong to the body,' it would not for that reason cease to be part of the body" (1 Cor. 12:16, NIV). What if your body were just one big eye rolling along in life? What a grotesque thing that would be. The body needs every member to fulfill its function. To the extent that members become inactive, the body becomes crippled.

Paul introduced the subject of spiritual gifts in 1 Corinthians 12:4-11,28-31. Gifts are given to the body through its individual members. Christians should be encouraged to discover and cultivate their spiritual gifts. They are to exercise these gifts to build up the body and to participate in the church's mission. A church has every gift needed to carry out the vision and mission of its Lord. The church should utilize the diversity of its members' gifts. To fail to do so short-circuits the power flow in the body.

Diversity is not only the dynamic but also the difficulty of the church. It is difficult for many members to realize their value to both the Head and the body. We tend to compare ourselves with others who excel. It is easy for us to conclude that because we cannot preach, teach, sing, or serve in a particular way, we can do nothing. Then we are engulfed by an attitude of low spiritual self-esteem.

One of the great needs of the church is to affirm every member's worth. The church needs to help the member understand: "God made you. You are the only you God made because God wants to use you as God can use no one but you."

Another part of the difficulty is the tendency to press everyone into the same mold. Acceptance of diversity is mandatory. Granted, some unique and even difficult people can be present in the church. Some may be quite difficult. But God uses unique, difficult people, too. In fact, it takes all types of members to do all kinds of ministries and reach all sorts of people. The church grows in its maturity and extends its ministry by expanding its circle of acceptance of diversity.

As a pastor, I had the privilege of leading to Christ a young man from a sordid background. Although he was saved, he had many "rough edges." He did not seem to fit anywhere in church. But he had a sincere, zealous spirit for Christ and for sharing Him. A Sunday School class accepted and nurtured him. He was gifted in reaching people from his old background for Christ and the church. Many trophies of grace came to Christ and into the church through his caring witness and ministry. It would have been tragic if the church had ignored him and had let him drop out because he was different.

As members experience unity in Christ and contribute their diverse personalities and gifts, the church becomes effective. Christ as Head fits the members of the body together to function effectively and efficiently: "From him the whole body, joined and held together by every supporting ligament, grows and builds itself up in love, as each part does its work" (Eph. 4:16, NIV).

Members of the body of Christ, in a way, are independent of one another. Christ leads each individual Christian personally. In your body your head may signal your right hand to act without your left hand. Likewise, our Lord leads members in their daily lives to minister and serve without the direct involvement of the rest of the body. The priesthood of believers is a precious truth. We can directly follow the leadership of the Head, understanding and applying His Word in our lives. This makes the church relevant to life. However, independence may be taken too far. A member should not develop an attitude that says, "The Lord is leading me so it's nobody's business what I do!" It is your business what I do and my business what you do if we are members of the same body. What I do affects you! What you do affects me! "We are members one of another" (Eph. 4:25). "There should be no division in the body, but . . . its parts should have equal concern for each other. If one part suffers, every part suffers with it; if one part is honored, every part rejoices with it" (1 Cor. 12:25-26, NIV).

Your head never sends a signal to your right hand to hit yourself in the nose. Both your head and your right hand are interested in your nose's welfare. If one is injured, the entire body experiences pain and difficulty. Churches need to learn and practice this principle. Members are interdependent. Each needs the other. Internal dissension injures individual members and the body as a whole. It diminishes the joy and effectiveness of the church. But as it moves forward with unity of spirit under the headship of Christ, a fellowship is developed that strengthens believers and attracts the lost.

PERSONAL LEARNING ACTIVITY 18

Place a *T* beside each statement that you believe is true. Place an *F* beside each that you believe is false.

____ 1. The church is the body of Christ on earth.
____ 2. What a church does outside its buildings and scheduled activities is not really important.
____ 3. Since Christ is Head of the church, the local church should seek His direction in all it does.
____ 4. The church is ruled by the majority. The church belongs to the members; therefore, they are in charge of the church.
____ 5. Every Christian has a spiritual gift that should be discovered, cultivated, and used in the life of the church.

The Church: Importance to Believers

In a conversation with an older gentleman I stated that every Christian needs to be an active part of a local church. He had lived an upright, moral life and claimed to be a Christian but had never become a part of a church. He asked: "Why should I become a member and be active in church? I feel that I am a Christian. I am all right as I am."

Many people today are asking that question. For those who are active in the church, those who have experienced meaningful church fellowship and understand the Scripture, the reasons are apparent and numerous.

Being added by God. Although individuals make decisions to join the church, our Lord adds the believer to His body when the believer is saved. The believer is to be baptized and to identify with the church (see Matt. 28:19-20; Acts 2:41; 9:18). The life of Paul is an excellent example. Before Paul's conversion he hated and persecuted the church. Immediately after his conversion he was baptized and identified himself with the church. When he went back to Jerusalem, the church feared to accept him. He could have easily turned away and rejected the church, finding his own way to serve Christ. But Paul persisted and, with the help and encouragement of Barnabas, was accepted by the church. Everywhere Paul went, he either started a church or sought out the church to help it grow and reach people. It is God's purpose for the Christian to plant his life in a local church and to share in its life and ministry.

Expressing Christ. Another reason every Christian needs to be a part of a local church is that an individual alone cannot fully express the person of Christ. But the church as a body, with its many members, can more fully manifest the life of Christ. What a privilege it is for a Christian to be a part of a church that expresses the glorious attributes of its Lord.

Caring fellowship. Every Christian needs the caring fellowship of a local church. One of a person's greatest needs is intimacy. A climate of love in a church enables members to give themselves to one another. A person's spirit of acceptance allows one to be open and vulnerable without fearing rejection. In such a context a Christian can better understand himself and come to grips with his inadequacies and character defects. Through the ministry of the Holy Spirit and fellow believers a Christian both receives the help he needs and gives help to others.

In an isolated life without intimacy a person can go on indefinitely without confronting his own attitudes and habit patterns. But as one lives in intimate fellowship, these become apparent through his relationships with other believers. Discipline is needed in the developing Christian life. A disciplining fellowship, characterized by Christ's love, provides the admonition and encouragement needed to gain victory over sins and sinful tendencies. Members give mutual support to one another. All of us are subject to temptation. Any of us may stumble spiritually and backslide. We need to belong to a fellowship of believers who care enough to confront one another honestly and to risk intervening to restore an erring brother or sister. Paul taught the Galatian churches to practice redemptive, restoring love: "If someone is caught in a sin, you who are spiritual should restore him gently. But watch yourself, or you may also be tempted. Carry each other's burdens, and in this way you will fulfill the law of Christ" (Gal. 6:1-2, NIV).

Without the discipline of accountability to a group of believers and to the body as a whole and without the gentleness of a restoring fellowship, it is much easier for a Christian to drift spiritually. Faithfulness to the church is essential to Christian growth. We tend to become like those with whom we associate intimately: "Bad company corrupts good character" (1 Cor. 15:33, NIV).

> He who walks with the wise grows wise,
> but a companion of fools suffers harm
> (Prov. 13:20, NIV).

All of us desperately need the nurturing fellowship of godly people.

Training and equipping. The church provides the training and equipping necessary for maturing in Christian living and service. Through preaching the Word, formal and informal Bible study, and discipleship training believers are prepared to deal with the basic issues of life and the temptations that will be faced. Gifts for ministry to others are discovered, developed, and utilized. In a church the believer is motivated and equipped for obedience to Christ's command to witness. Thus, the inner fire for evangelism is kept burning in the believer's heart.

Fulfilling Christ's mission. As a part of a local church the individual Christian is more fruitful in fulfilling the mission of Christ. The principle of synergism is a reality in the church. Much that could never be accomplished by an individual Christian's effort can be done by the body as it moves on mission together.

We need the church. Every Christian needs to be an active part of a dynamic, Christ-filled local church.

The Church: Privilege and Responsibility

To be a member of a local church involves both privilege and responsibility. Responsibility to the church goes beyond that of legalistic duty. It is the response of love and appreciation for Christ and His body. The church is called the bride of Christ. As a wife is faithful to her husband because she loves him, we desire to be faithful to Christ in every way because we love Him. A church member should consider it a privilege to be faithful in attendance. We want to come together with the people we love in the name of our Lord (see Heb. 10:23-25).

The Christian should strive to live a life that represents the Lord and the church well. The world's opinion of Christ and of the church is often shaped by what it sees in us. The church and its ministries should be faithfully supported by every member's tithes and offerings (see Mal. 3:8-10; 1 Cor. 16:2; Heb. 7:8). Tithing (giving 10 percent of one's income through his local church) and giving beyond the tithe, as God enables, are God's methods of meeting two important needs: the need for resources to carry on the work of our Lord adequately and the member's need to come to grips with one of his deadliest enemies, human greed. Faithfulness in tithing and giving grows as we learn to trust the Father. One can live more meaningfully on 90 percent of his income with God's blessing than on 100 percent living in disobedience and distrust. "God loves a cheerful giver" (2 Cor. 9:7, NIV).

Every Christian should serve our Lord in and through the life of the church. God has given gifts to each of His children to be used for service. Whether the service seems small or great, recognized or unrecognized, the Christian should rejoice to serve. Not every member can fill an elected position in the organization. But every Christian can serve through ministering and witnessing to others. Some of the greatest service that can be rendered is a caring ministry to other church members and to nonmembers. Every member can be an ambassador for Christ and for the church to reach people. Every member can reach someone for Christ and the church. Having a position is not the Christian's goal. If service to Christ and the church involves one in a leadership position, this is good. But the child of God already has the highest possible position and calling—being in Christ. The priority of the Christian life is servanthood, following Him as fishers of humankind.

The Christian should desire the church's advancement in mission for Christ. Consistent prayer should undergird the church's life. Daily prayer and Bible reading build not only the life of the person who practices them but also the spiritual life of the church. A praying church is a powerful church.

Conclusion
The local church and its work are central in God's great purpose of salvation. It will be accomplished! The church marches on to victory.

The future is sure. In spite of its opposition, regardless of its imperfection and critics, the church will be here waiting, watching, working, witnessing, and worshiping when Jesus comes. He will present His church "to himself as a radiant church, without stain or wrinkle or any other blemish, but holy and blameless" (Eph. 5:27, NIV). The church triumphant will reign with Him!

DOCTRINE IN LIFE

Take the following steps to apply what you have studied in this chapter.

1. Evaluate how effectively you are expressing your salvation in the life of your church. Include the following in your evaluation: worship, stewardship, ministry to persons in need, fellowship with other believers, and personal evangelism.
2. Decide at least one way you will better express your salvation through your church. Write down this decision and take at least one action this week to implement it.

---

[1]Paul Lee Tan, *Encyclopedia of 7,700 Illustrations: Signs of the Times* (Rockville: Assurance Publishers, 1979), 896.
[2]Darrell W. Robinson, *Total Church Life* (Nashville: Broadman Press, 1985), 16.

The Future Glory

QUESTIONS TO GUIDE YOUR STUDY
1. *In what sense is heaven the completion of the process of salvation?*
2. *What happens to a believer immediately after death?*
3. *What will the Christian's resurrected body be?*
4. *What will heaven be like?*

7 "I am going home in a few days" were words that conveyed the joy of the aged Christian grandmother to her pastor. She had been in a nursing home since her daughter could no longer care for her adequately.

"Oh, you are going home soon?" I asked. She did not answer. But she lifted her head and, with eyes that were alive with a glint of mischief and joy, looked heavenward and began to sing clearly and crisply:

> This world is not my home,
> I'm just a passing thru. . . .
> The angels beckon me from heaven's open door.
> And I can't feel at home in this world anymore.[1]

In a few days she indeed went home. I conducted the memorial service—a service that celebrated her home going.

Death for the Christian is not the dismal, gloomy end. It is the transition from the bondage of the earthly to the blessedness of God's eternal glory. It is a time when the child of God steps through the doorway of death into His presence.

The Glory to Come: The Completion of a Process
Salvation begins with the experience of the new birth, when the believer is delivered from the penalty of sin through the redemptive acts of

Christ's death, burial, and resurrection. Salvation continues as the Christian experiences the process of being delivered from the power of sin through the sanctifying, growing, keeping power of the indwelling Holy Spirit. Salvation is consummated in glorification as the Christian is delivered from the presence of sin and is received into heaven by the Father. Here our Lord is present with us. There we will be present with Him. Glory is ahead for the Christian!

The fullness of salvation from start to finish is God's glorious purpose for the believer. God enriched my life during a special time of need through the statement of a faithful, victorious Christian friend, Manley Beasley: "What God initiates, God completes." Manley suffered physical adversity and affliction for many years and often stood at death's doorway. But by faith he continued to fulfill his ministry of soul winning and encouragement to the glory of God and for the enrichment of many until the very moment God called him into His immediate presence.

From the moment one is saved, God continually works to prepare His child for heaven: "We know that in all things God works for the good of those who love him, who have been called according to his purpose. For those God foreknew he also predestined to be conformed to the likeness of His Son, that He might be the firstborn among many brothers. And those he predestined, he also called; those he called, he also justified; those he justified, he also glorified" (Rom. 8:28-30, NIV).

God continues to work in the believer so we grow to be more like Christ until He finally glorifies us in heaven. His work in us is much like the flow of the mighty Mississippi River. Its source is a small, trickling stream near the Great Lakes. It becomes a mighty river, emptying its waters into the Gulf of Mexico. It does not move in a straight line from its source to its mouth. Instead, it winds and curves around mountains and barriers until it makes its way to its destination. God moves in our lives, working in all things for good to accomplish His purpose. He works through the good and the bad; He works through the triumphs and the trials in our lives to make us like Christ.

Paul expressed his assurance of God's trustworthiness and power to glorify His people in heaven: "Being confident of this, that he who began a good work in you will carry it on to completion until the day of Christ Jesus" (Phil. 1:6, NIV). What God initiates, God completes. He has begun the work of salvation in us. He will not cease His work until it is finished. He does not leave us stranded. He never leaves the job half done.

THE DOCTRINE OF SALVATION

PERSONAL LEARNING ACTIVITY 19

The author quotes the statement "What God initiates, God completes." What do you believe this means in regard to salvation? Write your answer below.

_____

_____

_____

_____

_____

The Glory to Come: With the Lord

The consummation of our salvation will have two phases. Phase 1 will be in the realm of the spirit, when, at the death of the believer, the spirit is released from the physical body to be with the Lord (see 2 Cor. 5:1-6). Phase 2 will be the resurrection of the body at the coming of our Lord. The resurrected body of the believer will be reunited with the spirit, which has already gone to be with Him. Then we will ever be with the Lord (see 1 Thess. 4:16-18). This passage also indicates that there will be a generation of Christians who will not die. Alive when Jesus comes, they will suddenly be caught up to be with Him. They will be changed "in a moment, in the twinkling of an eye" (1 Cor. 15:52).

The questions inevitably come: What happens when the Christian dies? How does the believer's death relate to the glory to come? These questions are not new. The Thessalonian Christians asked them in the first century. Paul began his answer to them with the following words of encouragement: "Brothers, we do not want you to be ignorant about those who fall asleep, or to grieve like the rest of men, who have no hope" (1 Thess. 4:13, NIV).

Joyously in this passage we note that our hope in Christ covers even death. The death of a child of God is in the hands of our loving, gracious, sovereign Father. This truth became real to me early in my ministry when my wife died. We had gone through school together and had a four-year-old son. My wife had an incurable disease, and near the end of our college days her condition worsened. After graduation I pastored a small church and taught school. We were committed to serve our Lord and to reach people for Christ. In spite of her illness, she remained faithful in the church and in ministering to people until a month before her death. We longed for and prayed for her healing but always through the struggle committed ourselves in faith to Him, including in our prayers the words of our Lord "Nevertheless, not my will, but thine, be done" (Luke 22:42).

After a long period of intense suffering, early one morning as I held her hand, she drew her last breath. Sorrow engulfed my shattered life. The sorrow was real, but God taught me that we do not grieve as those who have no hope. I knew that her body slept in the grave, but I rejoiced in the confidence that she had moved from a body of pain and frailty into the presence of the Lord. I found that God has committed Himself to give us His highest and best. If He does not choose to heal, it is because He has chosen to do something better. There was nothing better for her than to be with Jesus. In my life God would work in all this heartache for my good and His glory.

At the funeral the pastor quoted Psalm 116:15, a verse that became a treasure for me.

> Precious in the sight of the Lord
> is the death of his saints (NIV).

As I researched this verse, several truths comforted me. Every Christian is a saint. The death of a saint is precious to the Father. It is not precious to us but a painful loss and a lonely experience. But such a death from God's perspective is precious. A loving Heavenly Father comes to bring His child home with Him.

The word *precious* means *highly treasured and greatly valued.* God so highly treasures and greatly values the death of His child that He never allows it at an untimely season but only when that life has fulfilled His purpose. The life of a Christian is in the hands of God. This is not determinism. It does not imply "Whatever will be, will be," and there is nothing we can do about it. It means that God is involved dynamically in the full scope of the life and death of His child. God views the totality of eternity from His omniscient perspective. When He sees that it is best, He calls His child to heaven. At times someone may pass unscathed through a situation that would appear to mean certain death. For another person the simplest difficulty can cause death.

The death of a child of God is so precious to Him that His presence is very real and near. He does not forsake His own but leads us through the valley of the shadow. One may be unconscious and unable to communicate with others, but God is there. His Holy Spirit communicates with the spirit of His child.

Death is the immediate transition from our earlier existence to the presence of God in heaven. Paul described it as his departure (see 2 Tim. 4:6-7). The word translated *departure* was used in New Testament times by sailors who loosed the mooring ropes of the ship and set sail for another shore. It was used by the Bedouins when they pulled up stakes and folded their tents to move to another place. Paul was ready to pull up stakes and move from earth to heaven.

At death one does not fall into a semiconscious state and spend eternity whirling around in a fantasy world. Paul knew that when he died, he would go to be with Christ. He was torn between his desire to depart to be with Christ and to remain to minister on earth. He said that he did not know which he would choose, though for him it would be far better to be with Christ. He knew that he would enter a relationship with Christ that was real (see Phil. 1:23-30).

Life in heaven is a continuation of the life we began on earth. There will be many differences, and all of the differences will be improvements. Yet the life itself will be the same life we received when we were saved. Some have the idea that eternal life begins when we leave this world and enter heaven. But eternal life begins while we are on this earth. Here and now we are raised up with Christ and sit together in heavenly places in Him (see Eph. 2:6). David possessed an overshadowing confidence that caused him to say,

> Surely goodness and love will follow me
> all the days of my life,
> and I will dwell in the house of the Lord forever
> (Ps. 23:6, NIV).

Physical death releases us only from the physical body. The release of spiritual life continues in heaven.

The transition of spiritual life from the earthly body to heaven is immediate. There is no such state as soul sleep. The body of the Christian sleeps in death, awaiting resurrection at Christ's coming. The spirit immediately leaves the body to take up residence in the eternal house God has prepared in heaven:

Now we know that if the earthly tent we live in is destroyed, we have a building from God, an eternal house in heaven, not built by human hands. Meanwhile we groan, longing to be clothed with our heavenly dwelling, because when we are clothed, we will not be found naked. For while we are in this tent, we groan and are burdened, because we do not wish to be unclothed but to be clothed with our heavenly dwelling, so that what is mortal may be swallowed up by life. Now it is God who has made us for this very purpose and has given us the Spirit as a deposit, guaranteeing what is to come.

Therefore we are always confident and know that as long as we are at home in the body we are away from the Lord. We live by faith, not by sight. We are confident, I say, and would prefer to be away from the body and at home with the Lord. So we make it our goal to please him, whether we are at home in the body or away from it. For we must all appear before the judgment seat of Christ, that each one may receive what is due him for the things done while in the body, whether good or bad (2 Cor. 5:1-10, NIV).

After death the Christian receives a spiritual body in heaven. There is no scriptural explanation or description of details about this body, which Paul calls our house not built by human hands and a building from God (see 2 Cor. 5:1). However, we know that it is a temporary provision of the Father until Jesus comes again to resurrect the believer.

PERSONAL LEARNING ACTIVITY 20

Paul wrote in 2 Corinthians 5:8 that Christians "would prefer to be away from the body and at home with the Lord" (NIV). What do you believe he meant by that statement? Does this verse speak to what happens to Christians when they experience physical death? Write your answers below or on a separate sheet of paper.

_____

_____

_____

The Glory to Come: The Second Coming

The Bible is clear that the second coming of Christ at the end of the present age will consummate our salvation. Views of the details and of the order of events surrounding His coming are many and varied. It is not our purpose to analyze such views; but regardless of one's personal view, some facts are scripturally clear and certain.

- Christ is coming again, as expressed by the direct words of our Lord Jesus Himself: " 'In my Father's house are many rooms; if it were not so, I would have told you. I am going there to prepare a place for you. And if I go and prepare a place for you, I will come back and take you to be with me that you also may be where I am' " (John 14:2-3, NIV). We also have the words of angels immediately following His ascension (see Acts 1:11) and of the apostles (see 1 Cor. 15:50-54; 1 Thess. 4:13—5:6; 2 Thess. 1:7-10; 2 Pet. 3:3-13; 1 John 3:2; and many others).
- At His coming the resurrection of believers will take place (see 1 Cor. 15; 1 Thess. 4:13-18).
- This present world order will end, with the elements melting with fervent heat and being destroyed by fire (see 2 Pet. 3:10-12).
- Judgment will take place (see Rev. 20:11-13). The wicked along with the devil will be cast into the lake of fire (see Rev. 20:10,14-15).
- A new order will be ushered in as God creates a new heaven and a new earth characterized by absolute righteousness (see Rom. 8:19; 2 Pet. 3:13; Rev. 21:1). Christ will reign forever, and His saints will serve Him (see Rev. 22:3-5).

The second coming of Christ is the blessed hope of the believer. Salvation will be consummated. The glory will be beyond description: " 'No eye has seen, no ear has heard, no mind has conceived what God has prepared for those who love him' " (1 Cor. 2:9, NIV). For the resurrected believer, at the second coming what has been promised and hoped for will become reality: "I consider that our present sufferings are not worth comparing with the glory that will be revealed in us" (Rom. 8:18, NIV). The glory ahead gives encouragement and strength for enduring trials and for continuing to grow in the daily Christian life.

The Glory to Come: The Resurrection of the Body

When Christ comes again with a shout that will awaken the sleeping bodies of the dead in Christ, the trumpet call will sound, and they will be raised again to meet the Lord in the air (see 1 Thess. 4:16-17). The resurrected, transformed body will be reunited with the spirit of the believer, who is already with the Lord. Those who are alive and remain will be caught up with Him and changed in the twinkling of an eye (see 1 Cor. 15:52). When Jesus rose, He became the firstfruits of the resurrection, guaranteeing that a vast resurrection harvest would eventually come (see 1 Cor. 15:20).

The resurrection body will be like the resurrected, glorified body of Christ (see 1 John 3:2). It will be fashioned for living in heaven, not bound by physical limitations of time and space. It will be perfect, without lingering effects of sin. We will be like Him! He is the firstfruits of resurrection. We will be the fruit that follows.

Jews celebrated the feast of the firstfruits at the beginning of the harvest. The firstfruits were gathered and brought as an offering to God in thanksgiving and in anticipation of the full harvest. It was a time of joyful celebration. The feast had a deeper spiritual application that pointed to the resurrection of Christ as the firstfruits and, then, to the resurrection of all believers at the second coming. Paul referred to the symbolism of the feast in teaching the reality of the believer's resurrection.

In presenting the truth of the resurrection, Paul anticipated the questions " 'How are the dead raised? With what kind of body will they come?' " (1 Cor. 15:35). In answer he illustrated God's power to create different types of life, listing examples of created life and bodies (see 1 Cor. 15:37-41). He included the created substance of plant life (vv. 37-38) and differentiated among the flesh of people, animals, birds, and fish (v. 39). Then he contrasted earthly bodies with heavenly bodies (v. 40). Paul's point is that God has given each created being a body appropriate for its nature, habitat, and function. The implication is that the same God who fashioned bodies suited for their present environments will also fashion resurrected bodies suited for heaven.

Bert Dominy interestingly says that in 1 Corinthians 15—

the question of *what kind* is approached by a series of contrasts between our present bodies and the body we will have in the resurrection.

1. There is a contrast between the perishable and the imperishable (v. 42). Our present bodies are subject to disease and de-

cay. They are mortal and will eventually turn to dust. Our resurrection bodies will be free from these limitations.

2. There is a contrast between dishonor and glory (v. 43). This does not mean that it is dishonorable to have a body. But our present bodies show the effects of sin. Our resurrection bodies will be unmarred by sin.

3. There is a contrast between weakness and power (v. 43). The most glaring weakness of our present bodies is their inability to resist death. Our resurrection bodies will be free from all handicaps and will not be subject to death.

4. There is a contrast between the natural body and the spiritual body (v. 44). Ray Summers points out that this verse is the heart of everything Paul said about the nature of the resurrection body. Summers writes, "Paul's insistence was that the eternal state will be a bodily state, even as the temporal state has been a bodily state. He did not say that there is planted a *body* and raised a *spirit.* He said there is planted a *natural* body and raised a *spiritual* body."[2]

The Glory to Come: Our Heavenly Home

Believers are vitally interested in their heavenly home. Sometimes life's circumstances make a Christian homesick for heaven, but even when God's people are not in difficult circumstances, such as sickness and suffering, they have a strong interest in heaven. People often ask questions about heaven. Some of these questions can be answered only from the standpoint of faith. Heaven is far more wonderful than anything we believe about it. But in our study of salvation it is appropriate to give some thought to our heavenly home, the believer's destiny.

Capacity for heaven. Believers will enter heaven as the same persons but as transformed persons to realize God's true purpose for His children. The persons we are at death or at the second coming of Christ we will continue to be in heaven. This life is the time for developing Christlikeness in character. All of God's children will be true children of God and will share the same eternal life, but we will not be of the same spiritual stature.[3]

Capacity for God and for spiritual experience is an important factor for life in heaven. Maturing in Christlikeness is central in our developing a capacity for enjoyment in heaven. A Bible professor illustrated this point by comparing the Christian life to containers. One person, having developed in Christian maturity, has become like a gallon container. Another has developed a life like a pint container. In heaven each will be filled to overflowing. Each fully enjoys heaven according to his capacity for spiritual appreciation.[4]

The development of a capacity for appreciating art illustrates this truth. To one person a great work of art may be just another picture. To another, whose interest, study, and experience have developed understanding and appreciation, it is a breathtaking masterpiece.

Through His overshadowing grace God is always at work in us and around us to help us develop and enlarge our capacity for Him. This is the work of salvation! How wonderful it is to live experiencing His presence now and to anticipate enjoying and glorifying Him forever. In the light of this truth nothing could be more important than for us to follow the admonition "Set your minds on things above, not on earthly things" (Col. 3:2, NIV).

Rewards in heaven. In heaven Christians will share alike in being filled with all the fullness of God. In this respect there will be no difference. We will all be perfected with the same Christlikeness to share in the same heaven. Each will be filled to the fullness of the capacity of his own spiritual life. However, another factor will affect our condition in heaven: rewards for the deeds done while on earth.

The fact of rewards in heaven is clearly set forth in Jesus' teachings and in passages throughout the New Testament. In the last of the Beatitudes Jesus promised: " 'Blessed are you when people insult you, persecute you and falsely say all kinds of evil against you because of me. Rejoice and be glad, because great is your reward in heaven, for in the same way they persecuted the prophets who were before you' " (Matt. 5:11-12, NIV). Again Jesus said, " 'The Son of man is going to come in his Father's glory with his angels, and then he will reward each person according to what he has done' " (Matt. 16:27, NIV). Paul echoed the truth of our Lord: "God 'will give to each person according to what he has done' " (Rom. 2:6, NIV). "So then, each of us will give an account of himself to God" (Rom. 14:12, NIV). He explained further, "We must all appear before the judgment seat of Christ, that each one may receive what is due him for the things done while in the body, whether good or bad" (2 Cor. 5:10, NIV).

Two questions arise as we consider rewards: What is the basis on which God will reward us in heaven? What is the nature of the rewards, or what types of rewards will He give?

Basis for rewards. True Christian service is that which is done for Christ to the glory of God. It includes the totality of life's activities: "Whatever you do, whether in word or deed, do it all in the name of the Lord Jesus" (Col. 3:17, NIV). "Whatever you do, work at it with all your heart, as working for the Lord, not for men" (Col. 3:23, NIV). Christ Himself is the foundation on which the Christian life is built, and how one builds determines one's reward:

> No one can lay any foundation other than the one already laid, which is Jesus Christ. If any man builds on this foundation using gold, silver, costly stones, wood, hay or straw, his work will be shown for what it is, because the Day will bring it to light. It will be revealed with fire, and the fire will test the quality of each man's work. If what he has built survives, he will receive his reward. If it is burned up, he will suffer loss; he himself will be saved, but only as one escaping through the flames (1 Cor. 3:11-15, NIV).

At the judgment seat of Christ every work will be shown for what sort it is. Rewards will not be given according to the amount of service rendered but according to the faithfulness of the servant. In His parable of the talents Jesus commended those who were faithful servants not because of the amounts they gained but because of their faithfulness in utilizing what He had placed in their care: " 'Well done, good and faithful servant!' " (Matt. 25:23, NIV). Likewise, He reprimanded the unfaithful servant for not doing what he could and should have done. Faithfulness is the key quality of stewardship and the final test in commendation for service.

The basis for rewards in heaven includes three characteristics of true Christian service. The first characteristic is motivation. The motive of genuine Christian service is love. The one quality above all others that makes service acceptable to God is love (see 1 Cor. 13), the God kind of love, giving oneself fully to and for another without regard for self. God looks at the heart and rewards the person who gives from a pure heart of love. But the person who has nothing to give, yet has the heart to give, will be regarded as though he had given. Many unknown saints will receive greater rewards than some who have received the world's attention and acclaim.

The second characteristic is intention. Intention is very near to motive yet can be distinguished from it. Intention involves the purpose of service. Jesus spoke in Matthew 6 of those who do acts of prayer and giving to be seen and praised by people. One may become involved in religious activity for recognition, material gain, or selfish enjoyment. The purposes of true Christian service are to glorify God and to influence others to glorify Him.

The third characteristic is that of lasting quality. Every work will be tested by fire to reveal its quality. Service that lasts will be that which God does in and through the Christian by His Holy Spirit. Jesus said, " 'Without me, ye can do nothing' " (John 15:5). Only the regenerate person can render acceptable service to God through the indwelling power of the Holy Spirit. God rewards such service in heaven. Such a person lays up treasure in heaven.

The story has been told that Pat Neff, the Christian former governor of Texas, was asked, "How do you lay up treasure in heaven?" Pat Neff replied: "You invest in something that is going there. The only thing going there is people."[5]

Christians serve God by glorifying Him so that people come to Christ and are saved. They glorify God by discipling, encouraging, and equipping persons so that they glorify God and lead others to Him. What joy we will have in heaven as we worship our Lord alongside those who are there as a result of our faithful witness.

Nature of rewards. The second question is, What is the nature of the rewards? How does God reward His children in heaven? Some will be ashamed at the judgment seat of Christ. Their temporal works of wood, hay, and straw will be burned up. But those who have built on the foundation of Christ will have lasting works of gold, silver, and costly stones as rewards. Some have seen these rewards as the crowns mentioned in Scripture: the crown of life (see Jas. 1:12), the imperishable crown (see 1 Cor. 9:24-27), the crown of rejoicing (see 1 Thess. 2:19-20), the crown of righteousness (see 2 Tim. 4:5-8), and the crown of glory (see 1 Pet. 5:2-4). What will be done with these crowns? Surely we will have such love and adoration for our Lord that we will join the 24 elders of Revelation 4:10 and cast our crowns before His throne.

In the Beatitudes Jesus said that true happiness will be our reward. In this life for the Christian, happiness results from being useful in bringing glory to God as we serve Him and others. On earth people look toward and long for retirement with a desire to cease from service. But the Christian longs for greater service to the Lord.

What will the rewards of heaven be? Arthur E. Travis aptly expressed it:

They will consist of *greater abilities, more opportunities,* and *greater efficiency* in rendering service to the glory of God. They will not be something that is given to the individual to have for his own personal benefit, but something that will enable him to give himself in a fuller sense. . . . God could not reward us in a richer way than by endowing us with greater abilities, opening up vaster fields of service, and in it all, supplying unlimited power to do the job perfectly.[6]

Realities about heaven. Ultimately, through His power in salvation God will bring His children into glory. The glorious culmination of salvation will be our final deliverance in heaven from the presence of sin. The Bible leaves unanswered many questions about the details of heaven and life there. Heaven is described through magnificent symbolism to convey to our finite minds its perfection and beauty. Its wonder far exceeds anything we can understand: " 'No eye has seen, no ear has heard, no mind has conceived what God has prepared for those who love Him' " (1 Cor. 2:9, NIV). We could not bear the many things Christ could have told us about heaven; therefore, He has not revealed these things to us.

It may well be that much knowledge of heaven would make us useless on earth. A traveler tells of returning home after a long voyage to a distant land. As soon as the sailors saw the shores of their own land, they became incapable of attending to their duties on the ship. Would it not be so with us if heaven were visible from earth? Its blessedness would turn us away from our duties. The sight of its splendor would so amaze us that we would weary of earth's painful life. If we could see our loved ones there, we would not be content to stay here to finish our work. Our Lord revealed enough about heaven that we may walk by faith with sustaining hope through the night of earthly life. At last the morning will break.

However, God has revealed definite realities about heaven. First, heaven will be a place, not merely a state of existence. Jesus promised, " 'I go to prepare a place for you' " (John 14:2). Christ Himself will be the central figure of heaven, living in our midst in His resurrected, glorified body. We will have bodies like His and will see Him as He is (see 1 John 3:2).

Second, heaven will be a perfect place. It will be a place of perfect holiness, happiness, and health. God will dwell with us, and we will be His people (see Rev. 21:3). The Bible gives seven "no mores" in heaven. There will be—
1. no more sickness or pain (see Rev. 21:4; 22:2);
2. no more hunger or thirst (see Rev. 7:16-17; 21:6; 22:1-2);
3. no more sorrow, crying, or tears; all cause for these will be removed forever (see Rev. 21:4);

4. no more sea, which is emblematic of unrest and separation (see Isa. 57:20-21; Rev. 21:1);
5. no more death (see Hos. 13:14; Rev. 20:14; 21:4);
6. no more night of weariness and separation (see Rev. 21:23-25);
7. no more sin; the curse of sin will have been removed (see Rom. 8:21-23; Rev. 21:7-8,27; 22:3).

The glory of heaven may be seen in what will not be there.

Third, heaven will be a place of perfect people. God's people will dwell with Him in perfect holiness. We will be made like Him. Our fallen, sinful human nature will not exist. Our self-centered nature will no longer be present to make us unhappy. We will be completely God-centered, living in harmony with Him. We will live with Him in perfect knowledge (see 1 Cor. 13:12). Unhindered fellowship will continue because God's perfect will will be done. Evil exists in this world because people are disobedient to God's will, but in heaven every thought, desire, and choice will exist according to His will. Jesus taught us to pray,

> "Your kingdom come,
> your will be done
>   on earth as it is in heaven"
>   (Matt. 6:10, NIV).

In heaven our relationships will be perfect. Broken relationships are among the most difficult of earth's sorrows. Not only will our relationship with God be perfect, but also our relationships with people will continue in perfect harmony. Our knowledge of Him and of one another will be full and complete. In Christ we all will be perfectly one in unity. In heaven our relationships will be on such a high plane that they will exceed the highest of those on earth.

There will be no distinctions in heaven. We all will be children of God. Jesus told the Saducees when they questioned Him about the resurrection and marriage in heaven, " 'In the resurrection they neither marry, nor are given in marriage, but are as the angels of God in heaven' " (Matt. 22:30). He did not mean that we will be angels but that we will be like them. Many interpret this to mean that male-female relationships, as we know them now, will no longer apply in heaven. Such distinctions will be overshadowed by our oneness in Christ.

In heaven we will be filled with appreciation for our Lord so that we will experience the continuing joy of worship and praise. Even we who have difficulty "carrying a tune in a bucket" will join with angelic voices in praise, singing, " 'Worthy is the Lamb' " (Rev. 5:12). We will serve Him with unceasing, perfect service. Some of our greatest disappointments on earth result from our inability to render what we consider to be adequate service to the One we love. In heaven the limitations of our service will be removed because we will be perfect people. No weariness will hinder our fulfillment (see Rev. 7:15; 22:3).

The beauty of heaven is indescribable. The Holy Spirit led John in Revelation 21—22 to write in symbolism about its beauty. He wrote in terms of the most beautiful things humankind knows. Here gold is precious and gorgeous. There it is transparent gold, covering the streets on which we will walk. The city of the New Jerusalem has gates of pearl and is constructed with the most precious stones.

PERSONAL LEARNING ACTIVITY 21

Cross out the statements about heaven that are false.

1. Heaven is a state of mind rather than a literal place.
2. Heaven is a real place that is perfect in every way.
3. In heaven we will no longer have to contend with a fallen, sinful nature because we will be perfect.
4. Relationships in heaven will continue exactly as they are in our present lives.
5. Heaven is beautiful beyond any description.

Conclusion
No matter how beautiful heaven may be, to be with Jesus will be enough for any of us.

> The Light of Heaven is the face of Jesus;
> The Joy of Heaven is the presence of Jesus;
> The Melody of Heaven is the name of Jesus;
> The Harmony of Heaven is the praise of Jesus;
> The Theme of Heaven is the work of Jesus;
> The Employment of Heaven is the service of Jesus;
> The Fullness of Heaven is Jesus Himself.[7]

DOCTRINE IN LIFE

Share your testimony of your salvation with at least one person this week. Use the testimony you wrote earlier as your guide.

---

[1]"This World Is Not My Home," *Old Fashioned Revival Hour Songs* (Winona Lake: The Rodeheaver, Hall-Mack Co., 1950), 4.

[2]Bert Dominy, *God's Work of Salvation* (Nashville: Broadman Press, 1986), 157-58.

[3]Arthur E. Travis, *Where on Earth Is Heaven?* (Nashville: Broadman Press, 1974), 35.

[4]Ibid., 36.

[5]Herschel H. Hobbs, *Studying Life and Work Lessons*, July-August-September 1969 (Nashville: Convention Press, 1969), 57-58.

[6]Travis, 66-67.

[7]Herbert Lockyer, *All the Doctrines of the Bible* (Grand Rapids: Zondervan Publishing House, 1964), 289.

Sharing the Good News

QUESTIONS TO GUIDE YOUR STUDY
1. *What example did Jesus leave to guide us in ministry and evangelism?*
2. *How do ministry and evangelism relate?*
3. *What stategies does this chapter suggest for ministry and evangelism?*
4. *Who is responsible for ministry and evangelism?*

8 Salvation has been provided! This is good news! Christ has accomplished all that needs to be done for humanity's deliverance from sin. Through Christ's death and resurrection He provided for humankind's full deliverance from the penalty of sin to full pardon and eternal life. He provided deliverance from the power of sin to growth and victory in the Christian life and from the presence of sin to life with Him in heaven.

God has placed His people in the world for a purpose. The church is His body, and every Christian is a vital part of the body. This implies that Christians are to do the work of Jesus in the world.

Being God's people in the world is not an easy task. As Christians we must pay a price. Paul wrote to the Colossians, "Now I rejoice in what was suffered for you, and I fill up in my flesh what is still lacking in regard to Christ's afflictions, for the sake of his body, which is the church" (Col. 1:24, NIV). What is Paul saying? Is he suggesting that Jesus did not suffer sufficiently to save? Not at all! Christ's suffering is fully adequate to provide salvation for every person. But it remains for us Christians, His church, to join in the afflictions of Christ to pay whatever price is required to take the gospel of salvation to every person.

We have already noted in this study that God's purpose for all humankind is redemptive. God calls all people to salvation. The power that makes salvation possible is the gospel: "I am not ashamed of the gospel, because it is the power of God for the salvation of everyone who believes: first for the Jew, then for the Gentile" (Rom. 1:16, NIV). " 'Everyone who calls on the name of the Lord will be saved.' How, then, can they call on the one they have not believed in? And how can they believe in the one of whom they have not heard? And how can they hear without someone preaching to them? And how can they preach unless they are sent? As it is written, 'How beautiful are the feet of those who bring good news!' " (Rom. 10:13-15, NIV).

God expects His people to be His witnesses in the world. Since we are His body, we are mandated to represent Him to all the people of the world. We must demonstrate concern, compassion, and willingness to minister and witness in His name.

Sharing the Good News: The Master's Example

Peter wrote, "To this you were called, because Christ suffered for you, leaving you an example, that you should follow in his steps" (1 Pet. 2:21, NIV). These words were written to encourage suffering Christians by pointing them to the example of Jesus, who suffered without bitterness or retaliation. An important principle is found here that relates to everything in the Christian's life: We can always find direction and strength in the example of Jesus. We can never go wrong if we walk in His steps. Since we are part of the body of Christ in the world, it is necessary for us to understand what He did to reach out to lost humanity. Then it is important for us to walk in His steps, to follow Him in loving ministry to people. The four Gospels offer a beautiful picture of Jesus in His earthly ministry. We find Him teaching, preaching, and healing; but most of all, we find Him loving people— all kinds of people.

Announced intention. We do not have to guess about what Jesus intended to do in His earthly ministry. He announced that intention early in His public work. Soon after His temptation Jesus launched a public ministry in Galilee (see Luke 4:16). Jesus' ministry in the power of the Spirit soon became a topic of conversation in the area.

Having returned to His hometown of Nazareth, Jesus was asked to read Scripture in the synagogue. When He stood to read, all eyes must have been fixed on Him. Unrolling the scroll of the prophet Isaiah, He found and read these words:

> "The Spirit of the Lord is on me,
> because he has anointed me
> to preach the good news to the poor.

> He has sent me to proclaim freedom for the prisoners
> and recovery of sight for the blind,
> to release the oppressed,
> to proclaim the year of the Lord's favor"
> (Luke 4:18-19, NIV).

Then he sat down. With everyone in the synagogue watching and listening, He said: " 'Today this scripture is fulfilled in your hearing' " (Luke 4:21, NIV).

It was no accident that Jesus chose that particular passage from the prophet Isaiah. He deliberately chose words that would set the tone for what He intended to do in the three years of His public ministry. In choosing this Scripture, Jesus aligned Himself with the great prophets of old who had cried out against oppression and had championed the cause of the afflicted. This focus in ministry was Jesus' announced intention.

Pattern of ministry. Jesus' entire ministry fit the pattern of the intention He announced in Nazareth. Jesus did many things in His earthly ministry. He taught as no one before or since has taught. He trained the men He had called as His disciples. He healed the sick who pressed in on Him day after day. He forgave those who were burdened with the guilt of their wrongdoing. Finally, He died on a Roman cross outside the city of Jerusalem. In all He said and did, the common denominator was people. He personified the heart of God for people—all kinds of people.

Jesus put people and their needs ahead of social and religious customs. For example, He ministered to the woman at the well (see John 4:1-26). The fact that she was a woman, a Samaritan, and a sinner did not deter Him. She was important to Him. Jesus put people ahead of religious rituals. He often healed on the Sabbath, which brought the anger and wrath of the religious leaders; but to Jesus, the sick persons mattered more than the Sabbath rules (see Luke 6:6-11). Jesus put people ahead of material wealth. He did not hesitate to heal a demon-possessed man, even though a herd of swine was destroyed in the process (see Luke 8:26-39). Finally, He demonstrated His supreme love for people when He died on the cross. He did not have to die, and no power on earth could have forced Him to die. The apostle Paul defined the purpose of Jesus' death in 1 Corinthians 15:3: "Christ died for our sins according to the Scriptures" (NIV).

There can be no doubt that Jesus put people first. It is important to note that He was concerned with people in their everyday needs. He did not just proclaim a message for people's souls. He demonstrated concern for everyday needs and hurts. If we are to follow in His steps, we too must be concerned about all the needs of people.

P E R S O N A L   L E A R N I N G   A C T I V I T Y   22

As Jesus related to people, He made them His priority. Review the preceding material and provide the missing words in the statements below.

1. Jesus put people and their needs ahead of social and religious _____.

2. Jesus put people and their needs ahead of religious _____.
3. Jesus put people and their needs ahead of material _____.
4. Jesus demonstrated His supreme love for people when He _____ ____ ____ _____.

Sharing the Good News: The Master's Mandate

The church as a body and Christians individually have a mandate from the Master. We are on mission in this world with Christ to evangelize and minister. Some people have created a false and dangerous dichotomy between evangelism and ministry, but such a dichotomy does not exist in the New Testament. It is a travesty to say that we are concerned about the spiritual needs of people while ignoring daily human needs. The kind of evangelism that does not care for the hurts, struggles, and deprivation of people is not rooted in the New Testament example of Jesus.

Matthew 25:31-46 has a powerful message for today's Christian. The picture is one of judgment, when God will divide people as a shepherd divides the sheep from the goats. The King will say to the sheep: " ' "Come, you who are blessed by my Father; take your inheritance, the kingdom prepared for you since the creation of the world. For I was hungry and you gave me something to eat, I was thirsty and you gave me something to drink, I was a stranger and you invited me in, I needed clothes and you clothed me, I was sick and you looked after me, I was in prison and you came to visit me" ' " (vv. 34-36, NIV).

The righteous will then express surprise at this commendation, saying: " ' "Lord, when did we see you hungry and feed you, or thirsty and give you something to drink? When did we see you a stranger and invite you in, or needing clothes and clothe you? When did we see you sick or in prison and go to visit you?" ' " (vv. 37-39, NIV).

The response of the King will leave no room for misunderstanding: " ' "I tell you the truth, whatever you did for one of the least of these brothers of mine, you did for me" ' " (v. 40, NIV).

This dramatic passage finishes with a condemnation of those who did not feed, clothe, visit, and minister to the King. The goats, those condemned, protest that they did not see the King with these kinds of needs. The response of the King is pointed: " ' "I tell you the truth, whatever you did not do for one of the least of these, you did not do for me" ' " (v. 45, NIV).

This passage conveys a powerful truth: When we minister to the hurts and needs of people, we minister to Jesus. When we fail to minister to the hurts and needs of people, we fail to minister to Him. He takes it personally. Ministry to everyday needs of people is not optional for Christians. It is unbiblical and unchristian to say that we are concerned about the spiritual needs of people while being oblivious to their daily needs.

But feeding the hungry, helping the poor, and ministering to the hurting people all around us are not enough. Evangelism is also essential. The word *evangelize* (*euangelizo*) means *to proclaim glad tidings.* *Euangelion* means *good news, gospel.* This is the message we share. *Euangelistes* is the word used for *evangelist* or *messenger.* Christians are messengers to take the good news to every person.

Our Lord clearly set forth the mission of the church during the 40 days of His postresurrection appearances to His followers. Each of the four Gospels and the Book of Acts record His mandate. Each presents a different occasion when Jesus revealed the priority of His heart, His purpose for the church, and its mission.

To the 11 disciples on a mountain in Galilee Jesus gave what has been called the Great Commission: "Then Jesus came to them and said, 'All authority in heaven and on earth has been given to me. Therefore go and make disciples of all nations, baptizing them in the name of the Father and of the Son and of the Holy Spirit, and teaching them to obey everything I have commanded you. And surely I am with you always, to the very end of the age' " (Matt. 28:18-20, NIV).

Every Christian is on mission for Christ. The Great Commission is Jesus' mandate for His church. The church is under Christ's authority. The armed forces of our country act under the authority of the president of the United States. The president's authority is great. But

Christ's authority over the church is greater. Christ is our Creator and Redeemer. We are His! He made us and bought us with the price of His own sinless blood (see 1 Cor. 6:19-20).

The Great Commission is a cycle. It begins with *go*, which literally has the sense of "as you are going." Go with purpose everywhere you go! Then *make disciples*. Teach to win people to Christ and to make them His disciples. A disciple is a learner and a follower of Christ. *Baptize* them. Lead them to crystallize their commitments in open declarations of love and loyalty to Christ. Through baptism they are incorporated into the church, which is Jesus' mission in this world. *Teach* them to obey Christ's commands. The primary command of Jesus is to go, make disciples, baptize them, and teach them to go and make disciples. The cycle continues until He comes again.

In the last chapter of Mark Jesus appeared at an unidentified place to the 11 again. "He said to them, 'Go into all the world and preach the good news to all creation' " (Mark 16:15, NIV). In the verses that follow (vv. 16-18), Jesus indicated that He will supply whatever is needed to accomplish this mission.

In Luke 24:46-49 "He told them, 'This is what is written: The Christ will suffer and rise from the dead on the third day, and repentance and forgiveness of sins will be preached in his name to all nations, beginning at Jerusalem. You are witnesses of these things. I am going to send you what my Father has promised; but stay in the city until you have been clothed with power from on high' " (NIV). "Again Jesus said, 'Peace be with you! As the Father has sent me, I am sending you.' And with that he breathed on them and said, 'Receive the Holy Spirit' " (John 20:21-22, NIV). Jesus came to seek and to save that which was lost (see Luke 19:10). If our hearts beat as does the heart of our Master, it beats for those who are lost.

Last words are important words! The last words of a loved one who is going away or is about to die are carefully weighed words. They are words of priority, purpose, direction, and emotion. And they are remembered words. Acts 1:8 contains the last words of Jesus to His followers before He ascended to the Father: "You will receive power when the Holy Spirit comes on you; and you will be my witnesses in Jerusalem, and in all Judea and Samaria, and to the ends of the earth" (NIV). Here is the strategy of the church to reach every person with the gospel.

Impossible! The task was overwhelming. Their number was so few. They were ordinary people from all walks of life. But they did what He said in the power of the Holy Spirit. Consequently, almost two thousand years later, we know, love, and follow Jesus. The strategy has not changed. It is as relevant today as the day Jesus spoke it to the church in Jerusalem. Yet the one thing Jesus said to do is the one thing churches and Christians often do less of than any other.

We must not see ministry and evangelism as competing strategies. The body of Christ is called to both tasks. It is a mistake to separate the two or to feel that they are mutually exclusive. Ministry and evangelism should be seen as one. We minister to hurting people because God loves them and is concerned with their suffering. We witness to people for the same reason. The term *ministry-evangelism* provides a helpful way to think about our responsibility to share our salvation. We minister to demonstrate the love of Christ. We witness to bring people to Christ. Our ministry must have no strings attached. It must not manipulate. At the same time, ministry must always witness to the love of God in Christ. Ministry must always call people to come to Him.

PERSONAL LEARNING ACTIVITY 23

Matthew 25:31-46 pictures ministering to Christ by ministering to human need. The passage mentions several categories of need, which are listed below. Beside each category write an example of the need for ministry in your community.

1. Hunger and thirst: _____

_____

2. Strangers: _____

_____

3. Clothing: _____

_____

4. Sick or in prison: _____

_____

Sharing the Good News: The Master's Strategy

In one of his excellent sermons Roy Fish, a professor of evangelism at Southwestern Baptist Theological Seminary, declared that the strategy for reaching our world is a go-tell strategy. It involves every Christian in witnessing for Christ. Christians are to go tell every lost person about Jesus. Fish further stated that today we are guilty of a subtle reversal of the New Testament strategy, having made it a come-hear strategy.

All too often churches depend solely on evangelistic events to attract the lost to hear the gospel presented. Conducting crusades, revivals, evangelistic events, and services are certainly needed. But they should be only part of a church's effort to reach the lost. If a church depends only on the preacher or evangelist to present the gospel, it short-circuits the power of New Testament evangelism. The mighty power of God is unleashed in a church and the multitudes are reached when every Christian is obedient in going and telling every person about Jesus. Inviting and attracting the lost to church meetings are important. However, the masses of lost people will never attend the church's meetings until someone has bridged the gap by going where the people are with the gospel of Christ. Many times this gap is bridged as the church reaches out in caring ministry to people in the community.

The New Testament pattern. The New Testament strategy of evangelism is a local-church strategy. Jesus gave it to the small local church in Jerusalem in the first century. Its mission field was the entire world, and its mission was to witness about Jesus in Jerusalem, Judea, Samaria, and to the ends of the earth. The Christians began where they were, in Jerusalem, lifting up and sharing Jesus. They were so filled with the Christ-life that it overflowed to all in Jerusalem. They shared Christ with every person, whether open or antagonistic to the gospel. The religious leaders opposed the witness of the early Christians, forbidding them to speak in the name of Jesus and threatening them with imprisonment or death. "But Peter and John replied, 'Judge for yourselves whether it is right in God's sight to obey you rather than God. For we cannot help speaking about what we have seen and heard' " (Acts 4:19-20, NIV).

The Holy Spirit did His mighty work to convict and convert multitudes through the disciples' witness. Even many of those who had participated in the crucifixion of Jesus were saved (see Acts 2; 6:7). The power of the gospel witness permeated Jerusalem, overflowed into Judea, spread through Samaria, and extended to the ends of the earth.

The gospel spread to Samaria and Antioch through the dispersion of the church, which resulted from persecution (see Acts 7—8). The sovereign Lord is able to use even opposition and antagonism toward the gospel to spread His Word and bring people to Christ. Christians do not go into a lost, hostile world as witnesses because they have been sent for. They go because they have been sent out and are accompanied by a risen Lord. The church receives its marching orders not from a world without God but from its Lord, whose strategy is to penetrate the spiritual darkness of the world with the light of His glorious gospel.

A local church was planted in Antioch, where the disciples were first called Christians (see Acts 11:26). They penetrated the area of Antioch with the gospel. Both Jews and Gentiles were saved. Under the leadership of the Holy Spirit the church in Antioch commissioned Paul and Barnabas to take the gospel farther into the pagan Gentile world. Paul, Barnabas, and their company won people to Christ and planted churches in the places where they went. Christians were dispersed and went everywhere evangelizing, winning people to Christ, forming congregations, and planting new churches. The churches became hubs or evangelistic centers for penetrating their areas with the gospel.

Paul spent two years in Ephesus preaching, reasoning, teaching publicly, and traveling from house to house, declaring to Jews and Greeks repentance toward God and faith in our Lord Jesus (see Acts 20:20-21). He won people to Christ and discipled and equipped them to do what he was doing. As far as we know, Paul never left the city during those two years. Yet Acts 19:10 says "that all the Jews and Greeks who lived in the province of Asia heard the word of the Lord" (NIV). The believers in Ephesus were equipped to share Christ. They permeated Asia, implementing the strategy of Acts 1:8. The church in Ephesus was a hub for evangelizing its entire area.

Local-church application. What is the application for local churches today? Leighton Ford calls this the strategy of total evangelism in his foundational book on evangelism, *The Christian Persuader.* He says that total evangelism is a strategy for our day.

> We are not seeking to invent a plan, but to discover God's strategy! . . . We must not confuse strategy with tactics. Strategy includes methods, but much more. Strategy involves *vision*—a clear-cut sense of what we are sent to do and the best principles of achieving our objectives. Methods can become tyrants unless

they are made the servants of strategy. This is why evangelism is always in peril of being stifled by the idolatry of one particular method.[1]

Ford says that the strategy includes three elements: goals, agents, and methods.[2] Our goal is nothing less than the penetration of the whole world. The church is to be salt and light to penetrate every stratum of a decaying, sin-darkened society with the life-giving gospel of Christ. For the agents to carry out this task, the mobilization of the whole church is required. The church should creatively employ every kind of legitimate method.

The local-church strategy of evangelism involves two primary factors: the total penetration of its area with the gospel and the total participation of its membership in witnessing. Total penetration grows from the church's vision to reach every person with the gospel. Just as the church in Jerusalem began its total penetration in the area of its location, a church today must penetrate its own area with the gospel. It should define an area for beginning, saturate that area with the gospel to create a God-consciousness and a climate for evangelism, and deliberately determine to discover every lost and unchurched person and share Christ with that person at the point of her deepest need. As this process occurs, the circle of the gospel witness will ever enlarge, just as it happened in Jerusalem. Total penetration will reveal pockets of people who need specialized ministries, such as language, cultural, and ethnic groups; poverty and affluent areas; institutionalized groups; and political, educational, and marketplace areas. It will result in beginning new ministries, starting missions, and planting new churches. Members on mission in the marketplace will permeate their work areas with the gospel.

True Vine Baptist Church in Oakland, California, was led by its pastor to claim its area for Christ. He led his small church to march around the perimeter, praying and claiming the city for Christ. Pastor Newton Carey, Jr., and his wife began to equip the members to witness and to win souls. They went out to reach the people. A transformation began to take place. Hundreds of lost people accepted Christ; the church grew bountifully in spirit and in number. The climate of the entire community changed.

In one church the WMU director led the women to reach the community. She led in equipping them to share Christ and to win souls. One morning 13 persons accepted Christ. Two women led to Christ four Korean men who spoke little English at the gasoline station where they worked. They and their families came to church on Sunday and made their professions of faith. They became the nucleus of a new Korean church, which soon had one hundred adult members. Total penetration results in starting new churches.

A commitment to total penetration will set the direction of a church. It is a mind-set! It causes the pastor and the members to view people with evangelistic eyes, seeing every person as lost until they know he is saved. A church on mission for Christ must have a people-reaching mentality. As it exalts Christ as Head and is filled with spiritual vitality, a church has His vision for reaching the lost and unchurched.

Total penetration of an area with the gospel requires the total participation of the membership in witnessing. Jesus said, " 'You will be my witnesses' " (Acts 1:8, NIV). The word translated *witness* is the Greek noun *martus* or *martur*. The verb is *martureo*. From it derives our English word *martyr*. The noun carries the idea of one who tells what he has seen, heard, or knows. The verb means *to bear witness or testimony.* The word *martyr* came to mean *one who bears witness by death.* A Christian's witness is to tell or share what he knows about Jesus. If a person is saved, he has something to tell about Jesus. The basic content of a Christian's witness is that he was a sinner, lost without Christ; that Christ died for his sins and rose again; and that when he repented of sin, believed in Christ, and received Him, Jesus came into his life to save. A Christian can share his experience of receiving Christ and can lead others to receive and commit their lives to Him.

Sharing the Good News: Every Christian's Responsibility

Witnessing is not an option. It is a mandate from our Lord. By virtue of who we are in Christ and who He is in us, we are His witnesses. By the life we live and the words we speak, we bear witness to Christ. It is not a matter of either living the Christ-life or verbally witnessing. Both are necessary! Either without the other falls short of fulfilling Christ's command. Our only choice is obedience or disobedience. Disobedience results in spiritual bondage and defeat in the Christian life. Obedience in witnessing enables Christ to become exceedingly real in and through a Christian's life. Christ promised: " 'Whoever has my commands and obeys them, he is the one who loves me. He who loves me will be loved by my Father, and I too will love him and show myself to him' " (John 14:21, NIV). It is unthinkable that we should profess to love Jesus and not desire to share Him with others.

A primary question facing Christians is, Who is to witness? The answer is found in Jesus' words: " 'You will be my witnesses' " (Acts 1:8, NIV). The *you* is plural. Witnessing is not the assignment only of the apostles, the pastors, the evangelists, and the specialists. Two major cop-outs are being used today to excuse Christians from witnessing. The first is: "That is not my job; it is not my gift. That is the responsibility of gifted specialists in evangelism." Not only is this the sentiment of many Christians, but it is also supported by some church leaders. This attitude is foreign to New Testament Christianity. Had the early church taken this view, Christianity would not have survived the first century. Witnessing is not a gift reserved for the few. It is the outflow of the Christ-life from within. It is obedience to His command from a heart of love for Him and for people. The gift of evangelism is given to the church, and a small percentage of Christians in a church may have this gift. Those who have this gift are to use it to equip *all* believers to win souls and to reap the harvest of souls for Christ. The gift of evangelism is to support the witness and soul winning of the body of Christ, in which every member is involved.

The second cop-out is equally lacking in scriptural support: "I do not know enough to witness." It may be, by emphasizing witness training, that we have left the impression that witnessing is a highly technical endeavor that requires intensive training. This fallacy needs to be corrected. A witness for Christ simply starts with what he knows and shares Christ with others. Indeed, one should study the Scriptures, pray, and avail himself of opportunities to be better equipped to win souls. But the place to start is where we are with what we know. Witnessing and winning others to Christ are primarily fires that burn within.

Those who are waiting until they know all that can be known about witnessing or until they feel comfortable will never witness. We do not have to wait until we have had a training course. Studies are helpful, but we also need to start now where we are with what we presently know.

John had been led to Christ in his home. On Sunday He came forward during the church's invitation time to confess his faith in Christ. That night he brought his brother and sister-in-law down the same aisle. He had led them to Christ that afternoon. He knew very little of the Bible, theology, and methods of soul winning. He simply shared what he knew about Jesus with persons he loved. New converts are often very effective in reaching others for Christ.

Witnessing cannot be relegated only to the pastor and perhaps to a few other specialists. The pastor must witness! If he does not, the people will not! The pastor is a model for the people in soul winning and ministry. He is an equipper. Through his preaching, teaching, leadership, and life-style, he does more than any other person to develop the climate and mentality of the church to minister in the name of Christ and to witness to His salvation. If the pastor does not have a life-style of witnessing and ministry, he will not be as effective in his preaching. Nothing can prepare the preacher's heart to preach on Sunday like winning someone to Christ during the week. The pastor must lead the church in evangelism and ministry.

However, the pastor and the specialists cannot do all the witnessing and ministry of the church. If they try, the purpose of the church will not be fulfilled. A church is to be a witnessing, ministering body, with every member sharing Christ. Every Christian is a witness. A church is filled with vitality as members, leaders, and pastor unite as a team to lift up Christ and reach the lost.

Total participation by church members in witnessing is the New Testament ideal. To move toward the ideal, the church must develop a conducive climate for encouraging members to witness. The emphasis and organization of the church must make equipping and engaging Christians in witnessing and ministry a priority. It has been said that a church must organize to evangelize. People reach people. A great force for evangelism in a Southern Baptist church is the Sunday School. The Sunday School is the church at work to reach people. Every department and class is an outreach unit. An evangelistic Sunday School provides the organizational structure, the equipping potential, and the support and encouragement necessary for maximal outreach. The Sunday School is the logical organization to discover prospects as members locate and identify every lost and unchurched person in a community.

Discipleship Training works alongside the Sunday School program to help believers grow and to equip them to become effective in ministry and witnessing to the lost.

Evangelistic urgency must permeate every aspect of church life if the church is to develop its membership as a witnessing body. The pulpit ministry, worship, Sunday School, Discipleship Training, Music Ministry, deacon ministry, WMU, Brotherhood, Recreation Services, and other components of the church's ministry must focus on the priority of witnessing and reaching people. Otherwise, members will tend to become involved in an aspect of church activity that they consider to be their service to Christ, without ever personally sharing Christ. When each organization and activity focuses on the priorities of exalting the Savior, equipping the saints, ministering in Christ's name, and evangelizing the lost, the church will approach the ideal of total participation.

A church can use many and varied methods to reach people. Some of these are revivals, crusades, evangelistic events, ministry evangelism, marketplace evangelism, door-to-door witnessing and surveys, and neighborhood evangelistic outreach. To be effective, all methods depend on the witness of individual Christians. Each church needs a continuing program for equipping members to witness and for involving every member.

A church should emphasize two types of involvement in witnessing. First, it should be involved in an organized program of witness visitation. Through it, members reach people who would otherwise be overlooked; new corners are reached; prospects are discovered; Christians are trained and equipped for soul winning; and the consistent practice of witnessing is established. Second, the personal life-style of witnessing should be emphasized and taught. Every member is on mission for Christ in the marketplace of life. Through consistent witnessing every day as we go, multitudes can be reached for Christ.

PERSONAL LEARNING ACTIVITY 24

Check the statements that you believe are true.

_____ 1. Winning people to Christ is primarily the job of the pastor, an evangelist, or another professional.

_____ 2. The pastor and other church leaders should set the example in ministry and evangelism and should work to equip all members to minister and witness.

_____ 3. Every Christian is on mission for Christ in the marketplace of life.

Sharing the Good News: Witnessing and Soul Winning

In this chapter the terms *witnessing* and *soul winning* have been used to discuss personal evangelism, witnessing, and soul winning. Some have made a sharp distinction between the two. The distinction is actually a matter of the extent of the witness. Witnessing may be thought of as sharing Christ with a person to the extent of that person's willingness to receive and to the extent of the Holy Spirit's leading. Soul winning continues the witness to its ultimate conclusion, guiding a person through the conversion experience and helping him to begin to follow Christ in discipleship. We may witness to a person but stop short of leading him to Christ. However, if we continue to witness faithfully, we will eventually have the opportunity to lead someone to Christ. Some have called this process drawing the net. Soul winning is a work of the Holy Spirit. No one except the Holy Spirit can transmit new birth. But we can be used by the Holy Spirit to persuade and guide a person through the conversion experience. A Christian should learn the skill of leading a person to pray, receive Christ, and make a definite commitment to Him. One never knows when God will give that divine opportunity.

I taught a soul-winning seminar in a fine church in a large city. At the conclusion a lovely, older woman waited to speak to me. Through her tears she said: "Oh, if only I had known this six months ago. My daughter and her prominent lawyer husband were separated. One morning he stopped by for coffee with me. With tears in his eyes he said: 'I need God! Tell me how I can know God!' I did not know what to do. I said, 'Jesus loves you.' I gave my Bible to him, and he left. Now they are divorced. If only I had known how!"

Sooner or later every Christian will have the opportunity to lead someone to Christ. The Christian singer Babbie Mason has written and has sung "Each One, Reach One." Yes! Each one can reach one, and what a joy it will be.

In everyday contacts with family, friends, associates at work, acquaintances at social functions, and neighbors Christians have opportunities to witness and win people to Christ. These are some of our finest possibilities. W. Oscar Thompson, Jr., a former professor of evangelism at Southwestern Baptist Theological Seminary, was writing the book *Concentric Circles of Concern* at the time of his death. His wife, Carolyn Thompson, completed the book. What a blessing it has been to many. It suggests a plan and gives guidance for beginning with those nearest in our relationships and extending the circle outward to witness to all those touched by our lives. Every person touched by our lives is influenced in some way. Each can be influenced for Christ. Relationships open a door to share Christ with every person with whom we associate. This approach has been called relationship or friendship evangelism. Although it has strengths, it also has two glaring dangers. This approach sometimes urges one to proceed slowly and virtually love the person into the kingdom of God. One person explained, "I simply try to model my Christian life and wait for the person to ask me about my faith." The first danger is that in the process of building a relationship, the person remains lost. Contact may be lost, an opportunity may pass, or the person may die without ever learning the way to salvation.

The second danger is that Christians may easily use this approach to excuse themselves for never sharing the gospel. Some Christian authors have written that intentional personal witnessing, especially in one-time contacts or door-to-door witnessing and surveys, repels people because a relationship of trust has not been established. Yet intentional witness is modeled throughout the Scriptures. The supreme example is Jesus. Time and again He took the initiative to evangelize through casual encounters. In just a few moments He moved from speaking about water to offering the living water to a Samaritan woman's spiritual need (see John 4:1-26). Early Christians also did this kind of witnessing. For example, Philip at the roadside intentionally witnessed to the Ethiopian and led him to Christ (see Acts 8:26-39). Intentional witnessing is Godlike. God was intentional in His purpose and provision of salvation. We must join Him in intentionally reaching people.

In relationship or friendship evangelism a Christian's priority should be intentionally presenting the gospel of Christ to lead the person to Him. Effective personal witnessing usually involves both the relational and the intentional. It may require three years to build a witnessing relationship. On the other hand, it may require no more than three minutes as the Holy Spirit does His work. It is not an either-or situation. Both are necessary in reaching people for Christ.

While on a trip to preach in a distant city, I stopped for a late lunch. To begin a witnessing conversation before I ordered, I asked Cindy, the server, the location of a nearby church. She explained how to get there. I asked if she ever attended. She said sadly, "No, since my mother died two years ago, I have had to work every day."

I responded: "I am sorry about your mother's death. It is tough to be alone, isn't it? May I share with you about how you can never be alone again?"

She took the witnessing booklet I had handed her and sat down at my table. I shared the plan of salvation with her. She prayed openly, although we were surrounded by customers and other employees. I gave her my card and asked her to go to the church, confess Christ, and give the card to the pastor.

Two months later, I heard from the pastor. He said that Cindy had come to him with her fiancé to plan their marriage. When he had asked them if they were Christians, Cindy had said: "Oh, yes, I am. A man sat at my table and led me to Christ one day. He gave me this card for you." The pastor led her fiancé to Christ and baptized both of them.

In one minute the Holy Spirit established a witnessing relationship so that I could lead Cindy to Christ. It is a mistake to limit what God can do. We need to capture every opportunity to share Christ. If the Holy Spirit has prepared a person's heart, she will be open. If not, we can share Christ as far as possible and leave the results to God.

It is helpful to realize that soul winning has at least three stages: the seed-sowing stage, the cultivation stage, and the harvest stage. Sometimes when we share Christ, we are sowing the gospel seed. The Holy Spirit cultivates the person's heart. Later, we or someone else will have the joy of the harvest when the person comes to Christ. At other times a person will immediately be ready to receive Christ. When this happens, usually someone else has earlier sown the seed, and the Holy Spirit has cultivated the person's heart and mind.

Jesus set forth the principle of sowing and reaping in soul winning in John 4:35-38:

"Do you not say, 'Four months more and then the harvest'? I tell you, open your eyes and look at the fields! They are ripe for harvest. Even now the reaper draws his wages, even now he harvests the crop for eternal life, so that the sower and the reaper may be glad together. Thus the saying 'One sows and another reaps' is true. I sent you to reap what you have not worked for. Others have done the hard work, and you have reaped the benefits of their labor" (NIV).

Perennially, the witness for Christ sows the seed of the gospel and reaps a harvest at the same time: "Let us not become weary in doing good, for at the proper time we will reap a harvest if we do not give up" (Gal. 6:9, NIV).

Conclusion

Faithful witnessing and ministry for Christ are not easy. Satan opposes them with all his might, waging a war to silence believers' witness and erecting barriers to keep us from sharing Christ. But a person who has experienced salvation is privileged to share the good news with others. Witnessing and ministry are not optional. They are part of a Christian's responsibility. God will help us overcome the barriers of unconcern, apathy, personal sin, and fear. He is able to make us effective. We are His people. The world awaits our witness.

Salvation is the purpose of God for all people. He continues to work in and through His church to reach all the world with the gospel. Let the church be the church—on mission for Christ, sharing the good news until Jesus comes.

DOCTRINE IN LIFE

Now that you have completed this study of salvation, commit yourself to the following actions.

1. Become a more active follower of Jesus through prayer, Bible study, fellowship with other Christians, and involvement in witnessing and ministry.
2. Use a prayer list daily. Include the names of friends who are unsaved and of persons who are hurting or experiencing difficulty.
3. Accept your responsibility to share your faith on a regular basis. Ask God to open doors of opportunity for your witness. Then make full use of those opportunities.

If you will commit yourself to these actions, sign your name on the line below.

Signed _____

---

[1]Leighton Ford, *The Christian Persuader* (New York: Harper & Row, Publishers, 1966), 43-44.
[2]Ibid., 44.

Teaching Guide
Don Atkinson

A study of *The Doctrine of Salvation* can be led by using one of three teaching plans.

1. The study can be led by using the resources found in *The Doctrine of Salvation—Teaching Workbook*. This teaching workbook contains overhead-cel masters, worksheet masters, discussion cards, and teaching-poster ideas. These resources are especially effective for large-group study, but they are also useful for small groups. The resources are designed to provide the study leader the necessary tools to lead an interactive, interesting study.

2. A pastor or another worship leader can lead the study in a series of Sunday and/or Wednesday evenings. The leader can divide the study into five or more sessions and can devote the entire worship-service time to teaching the material. One approach is to plan music for the service that fits the topic to be studied, to arrange for personal testimonies from individuals in the congregation about their salvation experiences, and to teach the doctrine. Pastors who choose this approach will find help in *The Doctrine of Salvation— Teaching Workbook*. The overhead cels are especially suitable for this type of presentation. Worksheets and discussion cards found in the *Teaching Workbook* will help involve participants in the study. The study should be taught rather than preached, and the involvement of participants should be encouraged. If the study is conducted during Sunday and/or Wednesday services, it is advisable to plan simultaneous studies for youth, children, and preschoolers. Study material for the doctrine of salvation is available for all age groups.

3. The study can be conducted in small-group settings. Adult Discipleship Training groups and home study groups will find *The Doctrine of Salvation* informative and inspiring. The study is also suitable for a retreat setting. This teaching guide is designed especially for that kind of study. The five sessions outlined in this teaching guide are designed for study sessions of between 50 minutes and one hour. This teaching guide is self-contained, enabling you to lead the study without additional resources. However, any of the resources in *The Doctrine of Salvation—Teaching Workbook* may be used to supplement this plan. Overhead cels 8, 14, 18, 24, 28, 32, 36, and 40, which outline the eight chapters in *The Doctrine of Salvation*, may be used instead of the flipchart outlines called for in the teaching guide.

Learning Goal

As a result of studying *The Doctrine of Salvation*, each group member should understand what the Bible teaches about salvation and the implications of these teachings for daily living.

Planning for the Study

1. Pray for the Holy Spirit's leadership throughout this study.
2. Secure necessary resources for the study, including a copy of *The Doctrine of Salvation* for each group member. The study leader may wish to purchase one copy of *The Doctrine of Salvation— Teaching Workbook* (item 5421-93). This resource will be necessary for the leader who wishes to use the overhead cels instead of making the flipchart outline called for in the teaching plan. The study leader may also wish to purchase *The Doctrine of Salvation* audiocassette tapes (item 4446-11) by William H. Stephens, which provide the study leader supplementary background material for preparing to teach.
3. Secure the supplies needed for the study, including a flipchart (or material to make one), large sheets of newsprint, colored markers, construction paper, masking tape, paper, and pencils. Bibles should be available for group members who do not bring their own.
4. Prepare a large poster by listing the five session titles on newsprint or poster board. Display this poster throughout the study.

The Doctrine of Salvation

Session 1: The Human Condition (Chapter 1)

Session 2: God's Eternal Plan (Chapter 2)
Responding to God's Plan (Chapter 3)

Session 3: The New Birth (Chapter 4)
Salvation and Daily Living (Chapter 5)

Session 4: Salvation and the Church (Chapter 6)

Session 5: The Future Glory (Chapter 7)
Sharing the Good News (Chapter 8)

---

5. Prepare a large teaching outline for each chapter in *The Doctrine of Salvation.* Each outline should be large enough for members to see it clearly. Consider using a flipchart, with the chapters outlined on one or more pages. A flipchart with blank pages can be purchased, or one can be made with sheets of newsprint. If you prefer overhead cels, you can use cels 8, 14, 18, 24, 28, 32, 36, and 40 from *The Doctrine of Salvation—Teaching Workbook.* You can easily write an outline of a chapter by finding the major headings and subheadings in the chapter. For example, the outline of chapter 1 is:

Chapter 1
The Human Condition

  I. Lost in Sin: The Human Situation
  II. Lost in Sin: Biblical Descriptions
 III. Lost in Sin: Consequences of Lostness
    A. In this life
    B. In eternity
    C. Descriptive words
    D. Certainty of hell
 IV. Conclusion

---

6. The room or area that will be used for the study should be large enough for group members to be able to move about. Chairs should be arranged in a circle or a semicircle rather than in rows. The meeting area should have a chalkboard, an easel for a flipchart (or an overhead projector if you plan to use the outline cels from the *Teaching Workbook*), and wall space on which newsprint and posters can be displayed. A small table will be needed for the leader to work from. It is best not to use a lectern. Sitting with the group will promote informality and group participation.

7. Plan the study carefully. Your planning should include preparing thoroughly to teach and carefully studying *The Doctrine of Salvation.* It is especially important for the leader to study the biblical material discussed in each chapter. Planning should also include discovering ways to involve group members in the study. This teaching guide will help you do so.

Session 1
The Human Condition
Chapter 1

Session Goal
As a result of participating in this session, group members will demonstrate an understanding of what it means to be lost by—
1. discovering biblical answers to the questions in "Questions to Guide Your Study" at the beginning of chapter 1;
2. making a list of lost individuals for whom they are concerned and will pray.

Preparing to Lead the Session
1. If you have not already done so, prepare the poster with session titles and a flipchart with the outline of each session (see "Planning for the Study").
2. Prepare to lecture on chapter 1, using the outline on the flipchart or cel 8 from the *Teaching Workbook*. Prepare carefully so that your lecture is condensed to no more than 20 minutes.
3. Prepare three large sheets of newsprint, with one of the questions in "Questions to Guide Your Study" in chapter 1 at the top of each sheet.
4. Prepare a half sheet for each participant with the following information.

Personal Prayer List

I believe that the persons whose names appear below are lost spiritually. I commit myself to pray for these persons each day this week.

Leading the Session
1. Welcome everyone. Lead the group in a prayer for God's blessing and leadership in this study.
2. Distribute copies of *The Doctrine of Salvation* and announce the study schedule.
3. Display the large poster that lists the study's session titles. Briefly

preview the entire study. Point out that this study is comprehensive and practical.

4. Write on the chalkboard or on newsprint attached to the wall the question *Why should we study the doctrine of salvation?* Allow time for group members to respond. Write responses beneath the question as they are given. Let the group choose several of the best responses. Discuss these briefly and suggest that they are the group's reasons for participating in this study.

5. Display the outline of chapter 1 on the flipchart or cel 8 from the *Teaching Workbook.* Briefly lecture on chapter 1, calling attention to the outline. Involve group members by asking individuals to read Scripture verses mentioned in the chapter as you call on them. Ask questions as you lecture and allow time for response from the group.

6. Divide participants into three groups. Give each group one of the sheets of newsprint with one of the questions in "Questions to Guide Your Study" written at the top. Instruct each group to take five minutes to discuss and answer its question. Reassemble the large group. Allow each group two or three minutes to report on its work.

7. Distribute copies of "Personal Prayer List." Ask everyone to write the names of lost individuals for whom they will pray this week. Allow about one minute for group members to start their lists. Suggest that they add names to the list as the Holy Spirit brings them to mind.

8. Select from three to five persons to serve on a panel in session 2 and ask them to meet with you briefly after the session. When you meet with them, ask them to prepare to serve on the panel by carefully studying chapter 3 in light of the questions in "Questions to Guide Your Study" at the beginning of chapter 3. Tell them that they will serve as a panel to discuss these questions at the next session. Assure them that the entire group will participate and that they do not have to be experts about the questions.

9. Encourage members to read chapters 2 and 3 before the next session and to complete the personal learning activities.

10. Close the session with a prayer for the lost and for the group.

Session 2
God's Eternal Plan
Responding to God's Plan
Chapters 2 and 3

Session Goal

As a result of participating in this session, group members will demonstrate an understanding of God's plan of redemption and of human responsibility to respond to that plan by—

1. identifying specific ways the Scriptures indicate that salvation is God's eternal plan;
2. answering the questions in "Questions to Guide Your Study" in chapter 3;
3. listing and planning to contact persons who helped them decide to come to Christ.

Preparing to Lead the Session

1. Study chapters 2 and 3 thoroughly and prayerfully.
2. If you have not already done so, prepare the flipchart outlines of chapters 2 and 3 or cels 14 and 18 from the *Teaching Workbook*.
3. Write the following topics and Scripture references on separate slips of paper.
   - God's initiative, 1 Peter 1:18-21
   - Christ in creation, John 1:1-3
   - In God's image, Genesis 1:26
   - All are sinners, Romans 3:11-12,23
   - Fulfilled in Christ, Galatians 4:4-5

   Plan to use these verses in your presentation of chapter 2.
4. Contact the group members you enlisted last week to serve on the panel. Remind them to read chapter 3 carefully and to find answers to the questions in "Questions to Guide Your Study." Remind them that they will serve on a panel to discuss these questions during the session.
5. Provide paper and pencils.

Leading the Session

1. After welcoming group members and asking someone to lead in prayer, write on the chalkboard or on newsprint, *Salvation is not an afterthought with God*. Ask members what they believe that statement means. Allow time for responses. Then explain that salvation has been God's purpose from the beginning.

2. Display the outline of chapter 2 on the flipchart or cel 14 from the *Teaching Workbook*. Distribute the slips of paper with key Scripture references.
3. Briefly lecture on chapter 2, using the outline and the key Scripture verses. Call for these verses to be read when appropriate in your lecture.
4. Display the outline of chapter 3 on the flipchart or display cel 18.
5. Ask those you enlisted for the panel to sit at the front. Tell the group that this panel will lead the study of chapter 3 by discussing the questions in "Questions to Guide Your Study" at the beginning of the chapter. Serve as the moderator by asking the questions one at a time. Allow group members who are not on the panel to ask related questions if they wish. This exercise must be completed in about 20 minutes, so move the group through the questions and do not permit the members to linger or digress. After the discussion, ask panel members to return to their places in the group.
6. Distribute paper and pencils and ask members to write the names of persons who influenced them to become Christians. Ask them: (1) to thank God for these individuals and (2) to try this week to contact those who are still living if they know where they live. Suggest that they do this in person, by mail, or by telephone.
7. Encourage group members to study chapters 4 and 5 before the next session and to complete the personal learning activities.
8. Dismiss with prayer.

Session 3
The New Birth
Salvation and Daily Living
Chapters 4 and 5

Session Goal
As a result of participating in this session, group members will demonstrate an understanding of the new birth and will relate it to their salvation experiences and to their daily lives by—
1. examining biblical truths about the new birth;
2. exploring the relationship between the new birth and daily living;
3. writing testimonies that relate the new birth to daily living.

Preparing to Lead the Session
1. Prepare carefully for this session. Make certain that you grasp the

material well enough to be able to summarize chapters 4 and 5 and to guide the group in the study activities.

2. If you have not already done so, outline chapters 4 and 5 on the flipchart or prepare cels 24 and 28 from the *Teaching Workbook.*

3. Prepare "keys" to Christian living from the section "Salvation: Keys to Christian Living" in chapter 5. To make each key, cut one page of heavy construction paper in the shape of a large key. Write one of the following phrases on each paper key: "Affirming the new nature," "Affirming fellowship with the Father," "Celebrating security," "Dealing with sin," "Following God's will," and "Living as disciples."

4. Prepare for each member a worksheet titled "Personal-Testimony Worksheet." Divide the worksheet into three equal parts: *My life before I came to Christ, How and when I gave my life to Jesus,* and *The difference Christ makes in my daily life.* Leave room to write a paragraph or two beneath each division.

Leading the Session

1. Welcome all group members and visitors. Pray for God's guidance in this session.

2. Display the flipchart outline of chapter 4 or cel 24 from the *Teaching Workbook.*

3. Ask members what they believe *born again* means. Allow two or three minutes for responses. Listen for any confusion about the term. Then ask why they believe the Bible refers to the salvation experience as a new birth.

4. Ask a group member to read John 3:1-8. Ask the group to respond to the following questions: (1) Who was Nicodemus? (2) How did he misunderstand what Jesus said about being born again? (3) Why did a man like Nicodemus need a new birth? (4) What do you believe Jesus meant when He compared the new birth to the wind? (5) What can we learn about the new birth from this passage of Scripture?

5. Summarize chapter 4, referring to the chapter outline. Use as many relevant Scriptures from the chapter as possible. This summary should take no more than 15 minutes.

6. Write on the chalkboard or on newsprint: *Conversion is only the beginning of the Christian life.* Ask members to explain what they believe that statement means. Allow two or three to respond. Explain that chapter 5 is about discipleship. Take a moment to explain the meaning of the word *disciple.*

7. Display the outline of chapter 5 on the flipchart or cel 28 from the *Teaching Workbook*. Summarize the content of each point on the outline.
8. Distribute the "keys" to Christian living. Ask two or three members to join each person who has been given a key. Allow five minutes for the groups to review their keys in the section "Salvation: Keys to Christian Living" in chapter 5. Ask each group to give a one-minute report on the key it reviewed. Explain that these keys to Christian living sum up the ways Christians should live their lives.
9. Distribute copies of "Personal-Testimony Worksheet." Ask group members to use the divisions on the worksheet to write their personal testimonies. Stress that the testimonies should be brief, with one or two paragraphs under each topic on the worksheet. If there is not time to complete the worksheets in this session, ask that members complete them at home and bring the testimonies to the next session.
10. Remind members to study chapter 6 before the next session and to complete the personal learning activities.
11. Close the session with prayer.

Session 4
Salvation and the Church
Chapter 6

Session Goal
As a result of participating in this session, group members will demonstrate an understanding of the relationship between salvation and the church by—
1. sharing their testimonies of salvation with another person;
2. studying biblical truths about the nature and mission of the church;
3. writing definitions of *local church;*
4. applying biblical truths about the church to case studies;
5. choosing one action to express their salvation better through their church.

Preparing to Lead the Session
1. Study chapter 6 carefully to prepare for a brief lecture on its content. Make certain that your preparation covers all the questions in "Questions to Guide Your Study."

2. Prepare the outline of chapter 6 on the flipchart if you have not already done so. If you are using cels, prepare cel 32 in the *Teaching Workbook.*
3. Write on a large sheet of newsprint the divisions from "Personal-Testimony Worksheet": *My life before I came to Christ, How and when I gave my life to Jesus,* and *The difference Christ makes in my daily life.*
4. Write the following case studies on separate sheets of paper.

Case Study 1

Sharon and Brenda, who are close friends, are talking. Sharon remarks: "I have missed you in church activities, Brenda. You used to be so active, but now you seldom get involved."

Brenda responds: "Well, to be honest, I feel that I can live my Christian life just as well without being involved in church activities."

If you were Sharon, how would you respond?

Case Study 2

Larry's pastor preached a sermon on the church as the body of Christ. He emphasized that every member of Christ's body has a function. Larry found this a new idea. How would you help Larry understand his function as part of the body of Christ?

Case Study 3

You are the chairperson of a special committee appointed by your church to plan ways to help new Christians become responsible church members. What would you include in such a plan?

Case Study 4

You are in a Church Council meeting in which directions for your church's ministry are being discussed. A difference of opinion surfaces in the meeting. One member speaks strongly in favor of the church's becoming more involved in ministering to needs in the community, such as hunger, homelessness, and abuse. Another member objects. He feels that the church should focus on preaching the gospel and meeting spiritual needs, leaving social problems to community agencies. With which member do you agree? Why?

Leading the Session

1. Welcome group members and call on someone to lead in prayer.
2. Ask group members to take out their copies of "Personal-Testimony Worksheet," which they completed at the previous session or at home. Display the newsprint with the three topics from the worksheet written on it. If someone forgot to complete the worksheet or was not present at the previous session, call attention to the three topics. Ask group members to find partners and to share their testimonies. Those who have not prepared testimonies should be encouraged to share as much as they wish with their partners.
3. Display the outline of chapter 6 on the flipchart or cel 32 from the *Teaching Workbook*. Briefly lecture on the chapter. Be certain to deal with the questions in "Questions to Guide Your Study."
4. Ask members to turn in chapter 6 to personal learning activity 17 and to complete it. Allow two or three minutes; then ask for a few volunteers to share their definitions of *local church*.
5. Divide the group into four small groups. If your group is small, members may work in pairs or individually. Give one case study to each group and ask each to deal with the assigned situation in light of the biblical truths presented in chapter 6. Allow 10 minutes for group work. Reassemble the large group and have each small group read its case study and give its response in 2 minutes or less.
6. Ask group members to turn to the section "Doctrine in Life" at the end of chapter 6. Call attention to activity 2 and ask members prayerfully to choose one action they will take to express their salvation better through their church.
7. Encourage members to study chapters 7 and 8 before the next session and to complete the personal learning activities. Ask for five volunteers to overview chapter 8 at the next session. When you meet with them after the session, assign each member one of the following topics in chapter 8 to overview at the next session: "Sharing the Good News: The Master's Example," "Sharing the Good News: The Master's Mandate," "Sharing the Good News: The Master's Strategy," "Sharing the Good News: Every Christian's Responsibility," and "Sharing the Good News: Witnessing and Soul Winning." Instruct the members to be prepared to summarize their topics in no more than two minutes.
8. Dismiss with prayer.

Session 5
The Future Glory
Sharing the Good News
Chapters 7 and 8

Session Goal
As a result of participating in this session, group members will demonstrate an understanding of the future glory that awaits Christians and the present responsibility of Christians to share the good news by—
1. studying biblical teachings on the ultimate completion of the salvation experience;
2. examining the relationship between ministry and evangelism;
3. exploring strategies for sharing the good news through ministry and witnessing;
4. accepting personal responsibility for sharing the good news through ministry and personal witnessing.

Preparing to Lead the Session
1. Carefully study chapters 7 and 8.
2. If you have not already done so, prepare outlines of chapters 7 and 8 on the flipchart or cels 36 and 40 from the *Teaching Workbook.*
3. Make copies of the Church Study Course form at the back of the book for all participants who are eligible to receive credit (see "The Church Study Course" at the back of the book).
4. Call the five group members you enlisted to overview chapter 8. Remind them that they are to summarize their assigned topics in two minutes or less.
5. Write the following headings on separate sheets of newsprint: *Ministry/Evangelism: What Are the Needs?* and *Ministry/Evangelism: What Can We Do?*
6. Have paper, pencils, and felt-tip markers available.

Leading the Session
1. Welcome group members. Call on someone to lead in prayer.
2. Distribute Church Study Course forms. Give instructions for completing them.
3. Instruct group members to turn to personal learning activity 19 in chapter 7. Ask those who have not already done so to complete the activity. After two or three minutes, ask for a few volunteers to share their answers.

4. Display the outline of chapter 7 on the flipchart or cel 36 from the *Teaching Workbook*. Lead the group in a 10-minute overview of chapter 7. Use the outline, appropriate Scriptures, and the questions in "Questions to Guide Your Study" to guide your presentation.

5. Display the outline of chapter 8 on the flipchart or display cel 40. Call on the five group members you enlisted to overview chapter 8. Remind them that they are to summarize their topics in two minutes or less. Allow the five members to present their overviews without interruption.

6. Display the two newsprint sheets titled "Ministry/Evangelism: What Are the Needs?" and "Ministry/Evangelism: What Can We Do?"

7. Explain that the study of chapter 8 has shown that ministering to people who are hurting or in need and witnessing to the unsaved are not optional but the responsibilities of every church and every believer. Ask the group to brainstorm needs for five minutes. Explain that brainstorming means calling out ideas and recording them without discussion or judgment. Ask someone to write with a marker on the needs newsprint. Call time after five minutes. Then ask the group to rank the needs. Duplicate ideas and those considered unimportant by the group can be eliminated. Narrow the list to six or eight. Follow the same process with the other newsprint sheet to identify between three and six actions by which group members can share the good news. Complete this activity in from 20 to 25 minutes.

8. Call on group members to make personal commitments to share their faith in specific ways. As time permits, allow members to share their commitments.

9. Ask group members who have met the requirements to turn in their completed Church Study Course forms.

10. Lead the group in a prayer of thanksgiving and commitment.

The Church Study Course

The Church Study Course is a Southern Baptist educational system designed to support the training efforts of local churches. It provides courses, recognition, record keeping, and regular reports for approximately 20,000 participating churches.

The Church Study Course consists of short courses ranging from 2½ to 10 hours in length. They may be studied individually or in groups. With more than 600 courses in 24 subject areas, the Church Study Course offers 130 diploma plans in all areas of church leadership and Christian growth. Diplomas represent hours of study, knowledge and skills acquired, and approval of the sponsoring agency.

Although the heart of the Church Study Course is leadership training, many courses are available for all church members. Each year adults and youth earn approximately 900,000 awards and 170,000 diplomas.

Originating in 1902 with two Sunday School courses, the Church Study Course now serves all church programs and is jointly sponsored by many agencies of the Southern Baptist Convention: the Sunday School Board, the Woman's Missionary Union, the Brotherhood Commission, the Home Mission Board, the Foreign Mission Board, the Stewardship Commission, the Education Commission, and the respective departments of the state conventions and associations affiliated with the Southern Baptist Convention.

A state-of-the-art computer system at the Sunday School Board maintains records for more than one million individual students and provides regular reports to participating churches. After participants enroll in diploma plans, diplomas are issued automatically as requirements are met. Credit earned in one church is recognized in all other Southern Baptist churches.

Complete details about the Church Study Course system, courses available, and diplomas offered may be found in a current copy of *Church Study Course Catalog.*

Requirements for Credit

This book is the text for course 05-096 in the subject area Baptist Doctrine. This course was designed for a minimum of five hours of study. Credit for this course may be obtained in two ways.

1. *Group study.* Read the book and attend group sessions. If you are absent from one or more sessions, complete the personal learning

activities for the material missed. Written work should be submitted to an appropriate church leader.
2. *Individual study*. Read the book and complete the personal learning activities. Written work should be submitted to an appropriate church leader.

To Request Credit

A request for credit may be made on form 725, Church Study Course Enrollment/Credit Request, and sent to the Awards Office; the Sunday School Board; 127 Ninth Avenue, North; Nashville, TN 37234. The form on the following page may be duplicated and may also be used to enroll in a diploma plan. Short-term Enrollment/Participation Record, form T-222, may be used to request Church Study Course credit, as well.

Within three months after completion of a course, confirmation of credit will be sent to the church. Copies of complete transcripts will be sent to the church annually during the July quarter if courses have been completed during the previous 12 months.

CHURCH STUDY COURSE
ENROLLMENT/CREDIT REQUEST
FORM - 725 (Rev. 1-89)

MAIL THIS REQUEST TO ➤

CHURCH STUDY COURSE AWARDS OFFICE
BAPTIST SUNDAY SCHOOL BOARD
127 NINTH AVENUE, NORTH
NASHVILLE, TENNESSEE 37234

Is this the first course taken since 1983? ☐ YES If yes, or not sure complete all of Section 1. ☐ NO If no, complete only bold boxes in Section 1.

SECTION 1 - STUDENT I.D.

STUDENT

Social Security Number | | — | | — | |

☐ Mr. ☐ Miss
☐ Mrs.

Personal CSC Number* ➤

DATE OF BIRTH | Month | — | Day | — | Year |

Name (First, MI, Last)

Street, Route, or P.O. Box

City, State | Zip Code

CHURCH

Church Name

Mailing Address

City, State | Zip Code

SECTION 2 - CHANGE REQUEST ONLY (Current inf. in Section1)

☐ Former Name

☐ Former Address | Zip Code

☐ Former Church | Zip Code

SECTION 3 - COURSE CREDIT REQUEST

Course No.	Title (use exact title)
1. 05-096	The Doctrine of Salvation
2.	
3.	
4.	
5.	
6.	

SECTION 4 - DIPLOMA ENROLLMENT

Enter exact diploma title from current Church Study Course catalog. Indicate diploma age group if appropriate. Do not enroll again with each course. When all requirements have been met, the diploma will be mailed to your church. Enrollment in Christian Development Diplomas is automatic. No charge will be made for enrollment or diplomas.

Title of Diploma	Age group or area
Title of Diploma	Age group or area
Signature of Pastor, Teacher, or Other Church Leader	Date

*CSC # not required for new students. Others please give CSC # when using SS # for the first time. Then, only one ID # is required.